Advance Praise for
Team Work

"People are the secret sauce of all organizations. In their new book *Team Work*, Russ and Rusty provide a guidebook for developing individuals into engaged and fulfilled team members resulting in thriving and successful teams."

—**Dan T. Cathy**, Chairman & CEO, Chick-fil-A, Inc.

"Being part of a highly performing team is a powerful experience in every imaginable way, but it is very rare in life to be a member of such a team—one that combines together so well that it makes achieving and success look easy. The core reasons why teams are dysfunctional are not secrets, but some people don't have the awareness and skills to contribute in a positive and productive way. This book *Team Work* will provide readers with a 'to-the-point' guide on how to be a great team member, how to create a functional team, and the keys to being a leader of such teams. Being part of a functional team or dysfunctional team is a choice—your choice. The messages in this book will show that there's really only one option."

—**Nathan Fa'avae**, Two-Time Eco-Challenge Winner
and Six-Time Adventure Racing World Champion

"Russ and Rusty share a vision to see people and organizations transformed through the powerful impact of servant leadership and high performing teams. Both leaders consistently prioritize team success and model personal excellence in their lives, uniquely positioning them as clear experts on the principles of teamsmanship shared in *Team Work*. Reading this book is an experience in active learning: each chapter is written with a winsome, practical, and inspiring approach, complete with reflection questions and action-driven challenges for the leader. *Team Work* outlines a clear and achievable path for helping people realize their full potential and truly thrive within their spheres of influence, and I am confident many lives will be changed as a result!"

—**Tammy Preston**, Executive Director, BlueSky Global

"Several years ago we partnered with Russ, Rusty, and the staff of WinShape Teams to invest in the lives of leaders in our company. At Shaw, we believe in developing people to be better both at home and at work, and WinShape Teams shares those values. People are our most valuable resource, and we are proud to trust the team at WinShape with ours. I am confident the principles Russ Sarratt and Rusty Chadwick share in *Team Work* can bring forth lasting change in any team."

—**Mike Fromm**, Chief Human Resources Officer, Shaw Industries

"Building productive, inspiring, and rewarding high-performing teams is a complex challenge. In *Team Work*, Russ Sarratt and Rusty Chadwick provide a comprehensive blueprint to help leaders and organizations create and sustain fulfilling teams. The thirteen principles are guideposts that unleash the potential of teams like we've never seen before. More importantly, the principles establish a legacy that future teams can build upon for generations."

—**John Oldham**, Assistant Chief, Jacksonville Sheriff's Office

"WellSpring Egypt has partnered with WinShape Teams since 2009. When they train us in team work, they help us to unite as one team to serve thousands of children in an amazing, effective way. Throughout our partnership, the word that is most visible and draws us toward WinShape is 'serving.' They serve us humbly and meet our needs despite the culture and circumstances. I am excited to see how *Team Work* will change communities around the world as these values have already impacted Egypt greatly."

—**Maged Fawzy**, CEO and Founder, WellSpring Egypt

TEAM
WORK

TEAM WORK

13 Timeless Principles for Creating Success and Fulfillment as a Team Member

RUSS SARRATT
AND RUSTY CHADWICK

 FIDELISBOOKS

A FIDELIS BOOKS BOOK
An Imprint of Post Hill Press

Team Work:
13 Timeless Principles for Creating Success and Fulfillment as a Team Member
© 2020 by WinShape Foundation
All Rights Reserved

ISBN: 978-1-64293-527-1
ISBN (eBook): 978-1-64293-528-8

Cover design by Joe Cavazos
Author photos by Jessie Morales
Interior design and composition, Greg Johnson, Textbook Perfect

FIDELIS
BOOKS
Post Hill Press
New York • Nashville
posthillpress.com

Published in the United States of America

2 3 4 5 6 7 8 9 10

Contents

A Word from the Authors

It doesn't have to be that way.

I wish I knew how many times we have uttered that phrase after encountering an unhealthy team or an unfulfilled team member. It has almost become a mantra in our work with teams around the world. A disappointed team member who feels left out of a decision. A frustrated leader who can't gain buy-in from the team. A collective goal never achieved. A relationship that goes from strong to strained. An individual who, because of a toxic or dysfunctional team culture, goes home depleted every day with nothing left to invest in the relationships that matter most. It doesn't have to be that way.

Having spent the balance of our careers learning and leading at a nonprofit called WinShape Teams, we have been blessed to work with teams of all sizes and industries. We have worked with some of the best teams in the world, and we have also worked with some pretty bad ones. We have met team members who are thriving and, unfortunately, many more who are not. While we know there will always be difficulty and struggles to overcome, we believe the life of a team should be hope-filled rather than hopeless. We believe a team should accomplish more than an individual. We believe teams should propel you forward rather than hold you back.

WinShape Teams has been developing stronger, better-connected teams and leaders since 1991. Along the way, we've pinpointed what makes for a healthy culture and happy people and put those findings into programs that have helped tens of thousands of people find purpose and clarity in their work. Our purpose is simple—build strong, healthy, fulfilling teams that change the world around them.

We wrote this book to share many of the lessons we have learned as an organization over the last thirty years. We believe work happens best in a healthy community and culture. Work should be a place where purposes are accomplished and people are fulfilled. This is why we strive to equip and inspire people to step from good to great and to make their work environment a place where people come alive as they work alongside others. We believe when you prioritize people and purpose, you bear the fruit of meaningful and sustained results.

You may think, "My team could never be like that." We believe it can. Your team can be healthy and successful, and you have more control over that outcome than you may realize. It all begins with you and a choice you can make to serve others, putting the team before self. This decision, and the actions following, can spark a new direction that changes your team forever. And it is not only about the team. Your personal success and fulfillment can grow as the team's success and fulfillment grows. In the end, we all win or none of us do. It is our sincere hope that this book helps you and your team "win" in all the ways that matter most.

Don't settle for an unhealthy, unproductive, unfulfilling, or even mediocre team experience. It doesn't have to be that way. Instead, let this be the beginning of something better than you ever imagined.

—*Russ Sarratt and Rusty Chadwick*

Chapter One

Teams Made Well

Class project.

When you read those words, what emotions and memories are evoked? While it depends on your actual experience, my guess is you can relate to some of the following situations. There is that one dominant person who tries to tell everyone what to do. They have an opinion on every single thing. They might even formally "appoint" themselves as the leader. Perhaps there are two who want to be dominant, and a power struggle breaks out from the start. Much of the conversation and group energy goes to figuring out who will have the final say on what happens.

Or maybe you are the only responsible person in the group. No matter how you split up the work, every time you get together you end up taking on a little bit more. Eventually you end up doing the project by yourself because you want to make sure you get a decent grade—even if that means getting no help from the group. Maybe you have one person who is never "available" for a meeting. You spend the entire time leading up to the project deadline just hoping they are pulling their weight.

Or maybe if we're honest about things, you are the one freeloading on someone else. You might justify things in a variety of ways. "The group will get a better grade if he/she does most of the work. That's what we all want, right?" Or maybe you think, "I'm so busy right now, I'll just have to lean on everyone else. I'll make it up on the next project." Whatever your rationale, you know deep down you are not pulling your weight.

Whether it is the class project scenarios described above or something different, many of us have bad team experiences from the past that can color our outlook on the idea of working closely with others. Teaming is not easy, and unfortunately, for many, being asked to join a team often brings to mind more dread than anticipation. "I'm going to be embarrassed." "This is going to be more work than the project alone." "I could do this quicker on my own." "Am I really going to be judged on the basis of someone else's work?" "Do I have to be on *their* team?" To many, teams feel like a chore. They are just one more thing to endure on top of the work that already has to be done. An initiative put in place by a boss who wants to pat him or herself on the back for introducing a team approach. They are slow moving, full of conflict, and induce a lot of frustration. And for what? To produce a mediocre result no one is really satisfied with. They are a "necessary evil," we think, and life would be better if they would just go away. These thoughts are not unfounded.

Teaming is tough because it involves bringing multiple personalities, perspectives, and approaches together. It requires us to put aside the freedom that comes from doing everything our own way and instead invest relational effort in creating alignment and moving forward together, which can be a heavy lift. It's true teams made poorly are a train wreck of frustration, stress, and angst. But it doesn't have to be that way; teams can be made well. They can be a source of immense fulfillment, opportunity, and potential. Teams done right are life giving, but they have to be done right.

What Is a Team?

Before we go any further, let's be clear on what exactly a team is. One reason teaming is so hard for so many is because what we often call teams are not really teams at all but just groups of individuals working alongside one another. I believe this is actually the root of many people's bad experiences. In their book *The Wisdom of Teams*, Jon Katzenbach and Douglas Smith use the term "working group" to describe a group of people who do not have all the characteristics of a true team. A working group doesn't have a team purpose or goals to bind them. A working group may need more time, understanding, or cohesion to make the jump to a real team.

So what exactly is a real team? There are almost as many ways to define the word "team" as there are teams in existence. An online search will give you well over eight billion results. Most of those definitions tend to involve the same ideas. A group of people. A diverse set of strengths or skills. A common goal. For the purposes of this book, let's put those three ideas together. A team is a small group of people with a diverse set of strengths or skills who pursue a common goal.

When you can start with a clear understanding of where your team is currently, you can form more appropriate expectations. Many times the conflict we experience in working with others comes from the gap between our expectations and reality. This gap is where conflict lives. We should not expect a group that is not a true team to automatically act like a team. While we advocate that a healthy team is often the best approach, there are definitely times where a team approach is not needed. You can still collaborate and work with other people, but your expectations can be much different. A clear perspective on your current situation may help you deal with any frustration that might be caused by your coworkers.

The core of this book, however, is directed to members of teams as we defined above—those small groups of people with a diverse set of strengths or skills who are pursuing a common goal. We want to see all teams become healthy teams, and we believe the principles in this book can help any team become more successful.

Purpose Accomplished; People Fulfilled

Having clarified what a team is, let's go a step further and define what we mean by a healthy team—a team made well. Healthy teams are different. They accomplish more than any one person ever could. In order for teams to be sustainably successful, two things must occur: the team must be accomplishing its purpose, and the people on the team must be fulfilled. Teams are not formed, or at least shouldn't be formed, simply for the sake of having a team. Teams are a tool, and tools have a purpose. So, a key measure of success for any team should be to what degree it is accomplishing that which it was formed to do. But this is only part of the equation. A team focusing only on performance may accomplish its goals in the short term, but if the team experience is not fulfilling for the members, this success will be short lived. Team members will either burn out, leave the team, or become disengaged and give less than their best. No matter how skilled the team members are, if they burn out, leave, or disengage, the team will never be high performing. Many teams struggle in one of these two areas. Really unhealthy teams struggle with both.

If you define success as accomplishing the team's purpose, most teams aren't all that successful for a variety of reasons. In our experience, many teams don't actually know, specifically, what they are trying to achieve. They show up to work each day and put in a lot of effort (maybe), only to see no tangible positive result at the end of the week, quarter, or year. People show up and do their jobs because that's what they are supposed to do. These teams have no measure for whether they are successful or not.

For other teams, though they may know the goal, they are just not able to accomplish the desired outcome. They complete lots of tasks, but their best efforts never lead them to the end result they wanted at the start. Other times, a team is just plain dysfunctional. These teams can't get anything done because they spend all their time dealing with relational, structural, or strategic problems. When they do complete tasks, it happens in spite of the team rather than because of the team. In each of the aforementioned cases, the common thread is none of them accomplish the purpose for which the team was assembled.

An even bigger issue for most teams is the unhealthy environment they create for their members—the people are unfulfilled. In these teams, everything feels like a struggle. These teams get labels like toxic or difficult or draining. These are teams where the team members work hard all day yet go home feeling even more empty, tired, and stressed than when they began. No one is happy. No one is satisfied. No one feels like their hard work is recognized or valued. Team members end up taking on a "me first" mentality.

A great example of this can be found in the movie *Remember the Titans* starring Denzel Washington. It is the true story of the T. C. Williams High School football team, the Titans. After years of school segregation in Alexandria, Virginia, T. C. Williams is formed in 1971 as the town's first integrated school. The movie tells the story of that first year through the eyes of the football team and its head coach, Herman Boone, played by Washington.

During the preseason, Coach Boone takes the team away for a mini-camp to learn the Xs and Os and build relationships within the team. At camp, the team's two best players, Julius Campbell and Gerry Bertier, who both play on defense, have several run-ins. While both players recognize the other's talent, they cannot get past their perceived differences. In a climactic conversation between the two, the tension boils over. Bertier calls out Campbell's selfish play. Campbell calls out Bertier's lack of leadership as captain. Campbell ends the conversation by saying,

> *Nobody plays, yourself included! I'm supposed to wear myself out for the team? What team? No, no, what I'm going to do is look out for myself, and I'm going to get mine.*

And there it is. When team members sense a lack of accomplishment, success, and support from the team, as Julius Campbell did, they default to self-preservation. And while team members in other settings might not verbalize their feelings this passionately to the team, the attitude Campbell adopted is a common response for the dissatisfied team member. Rather than working *with* others, they work individually with their own goal in mind, regardless of how it impacts the overall success of the team or the organization. Feeling no connection to the team and its common objective, dissatisfied team members see no personal benefit in sacrificing for the team, especially when no one else seems to be intent on sacrificing for them. In Campbell's situation, he thought he could focus on his role, work hard, and still see a path to stardom and a college scholarship. He shifted to an individual mindset, even though he was still technically a part of the team. Unfortunately, this happens frequently and can often spell doom for a potential team.

Better Teams Are Possible

My other favorite scene from *Remember the Titans* comes at the end. The team has overcome many challenges to bring together the divided town. This is most apparent in the relationship between Bertier and Campbell. Once at odds with each other, the two have become inseparable friends. Their mutual respect and care for each other serves as a significant catalyst for changing those around them.

The scene occurs in the locker room during halftime of the state championship game. The team is losing and the future looks grim. There are several factors going against the team as they come into halftime. The team's captain and best player, Bertier, was injured in a car accident earlier in the week. He is currently lying in a hospital bed, paralyzed from the waist down. Many on the team are struggling with the thought of their friend and leader back at the hospital. The team is facing their most difficult opponent of the season.

The team's play has been inconsistent in the first half as well. Their usual sharpness just hasn't been there. The most difficult challenge of all may just be a conspiracy to ensure they lose. Several from the state athletic association don't want to see an integrated team win the championship. As a part of the fix, the referees are clearly calling the game to ensure the Titans' opponent wins. All these factors contribute to the mounting despair and frustration of the team.

Coach Boone tries to encourage them to give their all and play their best. He tells them that whether the team wins or loses, they will be champions in his eyes because of how much they have overcome this season. Campbell, having taken the role of team leader for his injured friend Bertier, speaks up. He is not looking for moral victories. In response to Coach Boone's "do your best" offer, Campbell wants more.

> *No, it ain't Coach, in all due respect. You demanded more of us. You demanded perfection. Now, I ain't saying that I'm perfect, 'cause I'm not. And I ain't gon' never be. None of us are. But we have won every single game we have played— till now. So, this team is perfect. We stepped out on that field that way tonight. If it's all the same to you Coach Boone, that's how we want to leave it.*

The team went back out on the field for the second half, and their attitudes and play completely changed. The team went on to win the school's first state championship, and the first championship by an integrated team.

This scene shows how far Campbell and the team have come in their understanding of how a true team really works. The young man who was focused on promoting self now rallies the team to give their all—for the team. He understands the ultimate objective is the common goal of the team. Whether the team achieves "perfection" by winning the game is irrelevant. The team has been formed. Relationships have been built and deepened. Challenges have been overcome. The teammates truly care about each other, and their satisfaction is found in attempting to do something great together.[1]

And as is often the case, high performance on the field followed, and the team won the championship. When we focus on our own goals, our own desires, and our own benefit, the team suffers. But together, the team can accomplish more than the individual ever could. When all the players serve each other and the common purpose of the team, everyone wins. Teams can be healthy and life giving. Teams can accomplish their purposes and be fulfilling for their members. Whether your previous team experiences have been positive or negative, healthy teams are possible and they do exist. But they take hard work to build and hard work to grow. The beauty in the end is everyone benefits from healthy teams. Everyone shares in the success. Everyone partakes in the fulfillment.

Chapter Two

Servant Teamsmanship

How do you go about building a healthy team? Isn't that just the leader's problem? Today you can walk into any store that sells books, and you will find a seemingly endless variety of books on leadership. The market is saturated with books dedicated to leadership styles, skills, and theories. Some advocate for a strong, directive leader. Others call for a laissez-faire style allowing the team members to lead themselves with minimal direction.

Our perspective, defined as servant leadership, believes the best leaders are serving leaders. Based on the attention given to leadership, and rightly so, it would be natural for a team member to assume the only thing needed for team success is a good leader. A leader can lift a team to new heights or hold them back from accomplishing their goals. While a good leader is an essential part of a healthy team, team success (and individual fulfillment) is not determined by leadership alone.

The most successful teams have members who recognize they have just as much influence on the health and success of the team as the leader. The most interesting part of Katzenbach and Smith's work is the idea that what set apart the highest-performing teams is they were "deeply committed to one another's personal growth and success."[2] It wasn't that the teams spent more time together or worked harder at execution or had a better leader. They cared for each other more as individuals. We are not discounting that more time together, better leadership, and clear vision are all necessary parts of a strong team. Those are all essential characteristics. But the most successful and fulfilling teams genuinely care for each other, and that is something each team member can own. This care must be translated to action, and the heart of this action is service to others.

Servant Teamsmanship

We believe the success and fulfillment of an individual team member is directly tied to the success and fulfillment of the team. Imagine an experience where team members are committed to a common purpose and are willing to make sacrificial choices for the sake of the team. Team members help to carry each other's burdens. They care deeply about their teammates and want to see them flourishing in every area of their lives. This is what a healthy team looks like, and this kind of team experience is achievable. It happens when individual team members apply a new perspective to their engagement with the team. We describe this type of approach as *Servant Teamsmanship*.

Author and professor Jim Collins uses the concept of a flywheel to describe ongoing transformation in organizations. Collins points out how each small change builds upon the next. A flywheel is a huge circular object that is difficult to push at first. A lot of effort yields only a little movement. If you continue to push, the wheel gains momentum, which helps to turn the wheel. Pushing gets easier, and eventually the wheel continues to spin with minimal effort from you. Each push builds on the other to create the momentum that ultimately makes the wheel go. Servant Teamsmanship works in a similar way. One team member serves another, or the team as a whole. A relationship is built and strengthened, and a part of the work is accomplished.

The experience of success and the relationship with others builds a greater desire to serve more. As this pattern repeats, momentum is gained toward accomplishing the team purpose. The relationships built contribute to the team's personal fulfillment. When the team is healthy and successful, everyone wins. In this book, we will explain how an individual team member can intentionally impact their team through practicing Servant Teamsmanship. This approach is possible when team members begin to align the right mindset (beliefs) with the right actions (behaviors).

Establish the Mindset, Align the Action

Think back to Julius Campbell's attitude early in *Remember the Titans*. He was focused on self-preservation and self-advancement. As his mindset changed to focus less on himself and more on his team's success, everything else changed. We call this a "we all win or none of us do" mindset. The focus is on the team's success first and foremost. We sacrifice our own goals for the sake of common goals. While we may give input to those common goals, we believe the team's success leads to our success, not the other way around. Adopting a team-first mindset is not always as easy as declaring your commitment to the team. In the beginning it may take a daily fight with yourself to trust and give the benefit of the doubt to others. This is not a blind trust but an intentional change in your beliefs that's ultimately visible in your actions. You will see various references to the "we all win or none of us do" mindset throughout this book. Our hope is to point out the many times this paradigm shift comes into play.

A healthy team experience does not come from a mindset change alone. As our mindset shifts, the second avenue of impact occurs when our actions come into alignment with our beliefs. Our beliefs typically drive our behaviors. Our changes on the inside begin to show on the outside. Our behavior change reinforces the mindset shift leading to the behavior change in the first place, and the flywheel begins to gain momentum. We believe the behavior change part of Servant Teamsmanship takes two main forms. The first is Personal Excellence. We must pursue being the very best version of ourselves. The other part we call Sacrificial Service. A team-first mindset will lead to serving your teammates, and the common goal of the team, above yourself. We will spend the balance of this book discussing the practical ways you can change your actions to serve your team—for the team's benefit and your own!

To give an example of how the two parts of Servant Teamsmanship function together, we'll look to the world of music. In an orchestra, a large group of musicians bring together various types of instruments to collaborate and perform a piece of music. The orchestra contains multiple sections, each with a particular type of instrument. Within each section there are several different instruments of each type. The brass section might contain French horns, trumpets, and tubas, while the woodwinds include flutes, clarinets, and oboes. A conductor leads the group of sometimes over one hundred musicians to blend the individual styles and sounds of each section into a beautiful piece of art.

On their own, an individual musician and instrument can certainly play beautiful and inspiring music. Each musician can and must practice for hours to perfect their craft. However, their personal excellence can only carry them, and the orchestra, so far. To reach the full, deep, robust sound of a classical song, the individual parts must come together to form a new whole. The conductor must keep the tempo and shape the direction of the entire piece. The individual musicians must mesh with the others in their section. Each section must be woven together to tell the story of the piece to the audience. From the conductor to the musician with only a few notes to play, every member of the orchestra must come to the performance with the same mindset. We all win or none of us do. That is the only way it works. It matters less that a single violinist hit every note with just the right sound and speed. While that must happen, it matters most that the entire orchestra performs in sync, on time, and on pitch.

Your team is just like the orchestra. Every team member has a role to play. Do you and your teammates understand your role on the team? Every team member must be engaged and focused. Are you and your teammates in alignment on major issues? Every team member must be clear on the goal they are trying to accomplish. Does everyone on your team understand why the team exists? A team can accomplish more than an individual, but only when everyone is focused on the part they can play in meeting the collective goal.

Successful Teams

High-performing teams come in all shapes and sizes and from an array of different places. Here are a couple of examples that illustrate what it means to be a highly successful yet fulfilling team. These teams experienced success on the world stage and formed bonds between team members that were deep and meaningful.

First is the 1999 United States Women's National Soccer Team, one of the most successful teams of all time. The team won the inaugural FIFA Women's World Cup and changed the face of women's athletics in the process. The team was a mixture of gifted athletes who played the game at a level never seen before. What set them apart was more than athletic skill or endurance. They were dedicated to each other and enjoyed playing together like no team before them or since.

Sara Johnson, from espnW television, produced a documentary to celebrate the twentieth anniversary of the team's historic win. She found she "couldn't believe they could be that thoughtful, supportive, and in love with each other in real life. The '99ers were all about what was best for the team. There was no totem pole of importance. It was a culture of inclusion and celebration of every single person."

The '99ers, as their legions of fans called them, were successful as athletes. The team had multiple hall of fame–caliber players. There was a stalwart captain to lead the way. One of the greatest goal scorers of all time provided dynamic play each game. Tough defenders added a measure of strength and grit. However, more than anything a single individual contributed, the true strength of the team was the strength of relationships between each player. This team celebrated the victory together, and their success made them ambassadors of women's athletics to an entire generation. People began to look at female athletes differently, and many young girls were inspired to achieve their goals and dreams.

The second example is an adventure racing team from New Zealand, led by veteran captain and Eco-Challenge winner Nathan Fa'avae. Adventure racing at the elite level is a physically demanding endurance sport where teams of four travel from start line to finish line using a combination of trekking, mountain biking, paddling, and a variety of other disciplines. Teams must navigate the course using only a map and compass, finding a series of checkpoints along the way. A primary rule in adventure racing is that teams must stay together, always within sight and earshot of each other.

The clock doesn't stop, and teams often race through multiple days and nights with very little sleep. The New Zealand team, racing under the name Seagate, won the World Championships in 2012, 2014, 2015, 2016, and 2017. Then, in 2018, racing under the name Avaya, they won again. Obviously, they are elite athletes, but what makes them great is their commitment to putting the team first, even when it means making personal sacrifice. Describing the team, Fa'avae says, "I know from experience with adventure racing that to achieve what we have, you do have to put the team before self, and you need to be willing to work hard for the team, or even hurt for the team." Describing the team aspect of the sport, Fa'avae adds, "One of the great things about adventure racing that I think attracts us all is the team aspect, sort of the shared journey, the shared experience, and I think just spreading the load....When you are on the start line of a race as an individual, you really are there as a solo person doing your own thing, but when you are on the start line of an adventure race or a team event, you feel like you are part of something bigger."

This New Zealand adventure racing team is a particularly relevant example. In 2018, Rusty traveled with a film crew to Réunion, a French island in the Indian Ocean, to study this team during the World Championship race, a grueling multiday team endurance competition covering more than four hundred kilometers. He and his crew met the team, interviewed the members, and followed them throughout the race, observing and filming along the way. They learned a great deal about their approach to the sport and, more importantly, their team. In fact, what they found was so rich they traveled to New Zealand several months later to follow up, interview former teammates, and film additional backstory. They found the team's approach brought many of the principles in this book to life, and in the following pages we will share some of their story and their perspective with you.

Let the Journey Begin

For thirty years, WinShape Teams has been immersed in the world of teams. We train, consult, and coach thousands of team members every year. We have worked with lots of healthy, high-functioning teams, and unfortunately, we have also worked with a lot of unhealthy, dysfunctional teams. In the course of our work, we have seen consistent patterns emerge, and we also have seen the principles and practices common among successful teams. We believe with the right awareness, tools, and commitment, your team can be healthy too.

When thinking about teams, individuals matter. The kind of team we are talking about is only possible when individuals change their approach to team membership, and this book will help you do just that. In the chapters that follow, you will find thirteen principles for practicing Servant Teamsmanship; thirteen ways you can drive success and fulfillment for your team and for yourself. You will find personal examples from our own lives as well as very practical tips for how you can put each principle into practice. And you will also find specific applications for those serving as leaders and those who aspire to lead others down the road.

The concepts in this book will be helpful, but only if you put them into practice. Knowledge alone won't make it happen. Are you willing to try a new way of thinking and acting? A healthy team starts with you and your commitment to being the best team member possible, and that journey begins here. Take the first step; turn the page. Join us on the journey to becoming the best team member you can possibly be, and unlock the door to a successful and fulfilling team experience.

Principles
of Personal
Excellence

Chapter Three

Own Your Role

In early 2006, I (Rusty) relocated to a new city, and a friend invited me to run a half marathon in Nashville, Tennessee, later that spring. I had never been a runner, and 13.1 miles seemed like a daunting distance. But, always up for a challenge, I agreed and signed up for the race. A few weeks later my friend decided not to run after all. My training partner was gone, and I wasn't exactly a member of the local running club. I was new to town, new to distance running, and I felt like I was in way over my head. I needed a plan.

After a bit of searching online, I found a detailed training schedule that fit both my ability level (low) and the time frame I had before the big race. It gave specific instructions on when to run, how far to go, and when to rest. I knew in my current state I was wholly unprepared to run four or five miles, let alone thirteen. I also knew that come race day there would be nowhere to hide; I would reach the finish line or I wouldn't. I was determined to be ready, and I followed that training plan to a T. For the next ten weeks, I diligently ran the prescribed mileage—alone.

The weekend before the race, I set off on my final training exercise before the big event, a ten-mile run. For reasons I still can't fully explain, I chose to tackle this run at the local high school track—forty laps all by myself. It was not a pleasant experience. I finished—barely—but whatever was to come in the race, I knew I did everything I could to prepare. I was ready to give it my best.

The next week, I found myself nervously standing alongside twenty thousand others at the starting line in Nashville, totally unsure of what to expect. I had two goals: the first was to complete the whole race without stopping to walk, and the second was to finish in under two hours. One hour and forty-seven minutes later, I crossed the finish line and was overcome with the feeling of fulfillment that only comes from working hard and reaping the reward. There have been many times in my life when I have taken shortcuts, given up, or failed to properly prepare, but that moment in Nashville was not one of them. In that moment, I tasted the sweetness of giving everything I had to achieve the goal and then following through.

As I reflect on that race and the weeks leading up to it, there is one concept that stands out—*ownership*. It was my goal, my preparation, and ultimately my effort that would get me across the finish line. I felt a strong connection to the goal. I took ownership of the objective and the process of achieving it, and that ownership drove me to prepare well and give my best effort. This is often the reality when we operate as individual contributors. Ownership comes naturally because we are in the spotlight; we stand on our own performance, good or bad, and we are judged by the results we produce.

The reality can be quite different in teams. Teams have the potential to accomplish results exponentially greater than the collective efforts of individual contributors, but that potential is often unrealized. Teams can become a place for members to hide and underperform because their individual efforts are less visible. When individual team members hold back, giving only minimal effort, the result is the mediocre or even poor performance plaguing so many teams. The degree to which team members take individual ownership of their roles is a primary factor in how well the team will perform. If anything is held back by one, either someone carries the extra load or the work doesn't get done. Either way, it's not good, but it doesn't have to be that way.

The best way to serve any team you join is to *own your role* as a team member in the same way you take ownership for an individual goal or project. On healthy teams, each member has a defined role and clear responsibilities that contribute to the team's desired outcome. In less healthy teams, roles and responsibilities may be vague, meaning the first step toward owning your role is to seek clarity. Whatever the current state, the goal is the same: teams are at their best when every member gives their all for the collective goal, and this begins with personal responsibility and a commitment to excellence at the individual level.

Most of us have been on teams with passive participants who look to others on the team to carry the lion's share of the load and are quick to blame others when performance is poor. If we are honest, we have probably approached some teams this way. But what if every member of every team viewed their contributions as vital to team success and actively pursued excellence? What if every member focused on performing in their role versus simply existing?

You and I can't control how every team member approaches his or her role on the team, but we can control the approach we take. And by owning our roles, we can set the pace for those around us. But how? What does it mean to truly take ownership of our role on a team? There are three basic actions you can take in any team to own your role, and the first is to focus on creating value.

Focus On Creating Value

Owning your role is about being an active contributor to the team as opposed to a passive participant; it is about creating value. Your role on the team has a purpose, and it is not to be the sixth person on a six-person team. Owning your role begins with viewing your contributions as vital to the team's success and choosing to play your part in moving the team forward. Think about the best teams you have been on or observed. There are no throwaway members, no hitchhikers. Teams don't need people who are just along for the ride. Either you are adding value to the team or you are holding the team back, taking the team's resources without putting them to good use. The team does not exist for you, but rather your role on the team exists to help achieve the common goal toward which the team is working.

But here's the great part. While the team does not exist for its members, that is not to say there will not be individual benefit. Creating value for a team is incredibly rewarding, and certainly more so than coasting along while others carry the load. Much like giving a gift is often more gratifying than receiving one, pouring your effort into a team goal alongside others who are doing the same is very fulfilling. Think of any time a sports team wins a championship. The first thing they do is run toward each other and join in a team celebration. There is a shared joy and excitement they all feel because they know their individual efforts have helped produce a team result.

Be Prepared

As important as it is to focus on creating value, it is difficult to do so if you are not properly prepared. Individual preparation is a powerful way to serve a team and the common goal it is pursuing. In a prerace interview at the 2018 Adventure Racing World Championships, an extreme endurance event where teams of four trek, bike, and paddle over four hundred kilometers, six-time world champion and captain of the New Zealand team Nathan Fa'avae told me the following about preparation: "I think another layer of the trust that we have in our team is that people prepare for the race honorably or to the expected level. We come here to be ultracompetitive and ultimately win the world title. We live in different parts of the country [New Zealand] so it comes down to the individual to get themselves ready, to do the training, so we just have to trust that as we are out there doing our own training that our teammates are actually out there doing their own training as well."

He went on to say some racers romanticize the big race and enjoy coming to participate, but they don't put in the time on the front end to prepare, and this lack of preparation is exposed on the racecourse. Nathan's perspective highlights a principle true for all types of teams, including teams at work. To be our best when the team is together, we must do the more mundane work when we are by ourselves.

Why is preparation so important? In teams, a failure to prepare means you will not only underperform individually, but you will stunt the team's performance as well. How many times have you arrived at a meeting without reviewing the agenda, failed to complete action items, or neglected to properly prepare for a thoughtful discussion? We've all been there. I know I have. We get busy, distracted, or engaged in other priorities, and we end up coming to the team ill-equipped to contribute in a meaningful way. [When you fail to prepare, the team's focus must shift from achieving the goal at hand to helping you, the unprepared teammate, catch up, which affects not only performance but team morale as well.]

The good news is preparation doesn't require better leadership or more resources. It is not contingent upon the commitment or effort of others. Being prepared is an individual decision each of us can make every day, and that should be very empowering. In a work context, this may mean reviewing meeting agendas and putting intentional thought toward topics on which you can add value, disciplining yourself to complete action items in the agreed-upon time frame, or conducting research or prework that will help move the team forward more quickly when everyone comes together. Even when your individual contributions will not be distinguishable in the final product, take ownership of the team outcome and prepare well.

Additionally, being prepared goes beyond the things you do to specifically get ready for the work you do on the team. It also means practicing good self-care. It is difficult to own your role and perform well for the team when you are not showing up at your personal best. The way you care for your physical, mental, spiritual, and emotional health will certainly have an impact on your ability to serve your team. This means an intentional approach to your morning routine, exercise, sleep, nutrition, family time, vacation, and much more are all part of the preparation process. Investing well here is a great way to care for your team and yourself.

Take Initiative

Once you have purposed to create value and put in the time to prepare, the next way to own your role is to take initiative. Ownership brings a sense of responsibility, and responsibility drives action. High performance on a team never happens when the members sit back and wait for others to act first. When everyone takes that posture, you can imagine how little movement occurs. You've seen this on teams before. Everyone is waiting for someone else to move and believing they can't do their job until someone else acts. Taking initiative means breaking this cycle. It means developing a bias for action based on an understanding that the team needs you to be bold and courageous, willing to take ownership of the role you've been given and the responsibilities it requires.

I've had many conversations over the years with people who are frustrated because they are waiting for someone to make a decision, craft a plan, or solve a problem. They feel like they don't have control over the situation and there is nothing they can do—they feel stuck. In my experience, it is rarely the case individuals have as little control as they think. In most situations, there is much you and I can do to move the ball forward, and those team members who look for ways to act, rather than bemoaning the inaction of others, provide an important service to their teams. Too often we are content to wait for the leader to give direction or for someone else to move, all the while using the inaction of others to justify our lack of engagement. Most of the time we have significantly more influence than we realize, and acting or humbly seeking clarity from the team and its leader could be the thing that initiates momentum toward desired results.

Taking initiative can be done in a variety of ways. It might include asking for resources from both the leader and the team to ensure you have what you need to be successful. It could be stepping up to make suggestions and propose solutions to problems rather than pointing fingers or waiting for others. Taking initiative means putting ideas on the table before you have a perfect plan and being willing to try new things.

Seeking clarity from the team and the leader regarding the team's purpose and goals is a specific way to take initiative that warrants highlighting. Perhaps the most important reason we hold back in the team context is a lack of connection to the team's purpose. If we either don't know or don't value the work the team is doing, it becomes much easier to drift along doing only enough to get by. As a team member, you may not be responsible for developing the purpose of the team, but you can and should seek clarity on that purpose when it is unclear or unspoken.

Closing Thought

Choosing to own your role is a foundational step to helping your team reach its full potential and finding more fulfillment for yourself along the way. What the team needs from you first and foremost is personal excellence in the role you have been given. Then, once you are owning your own role, you can look to step beyond your responsibilities to add value in new ways and help others succeed. We often use the phrase "go the extra mile" in reference to doing more than is required, but it is important to remember that going the extra mile is only valuable if we go the required mile first.

Best Practices/Reminders

- Review meeting agendas and consider discussion topics prior to attending team meetings.
- Complete action items. (This sounds simple, but how often do we make excuses for why action items are delayed?)
- Evaluate your daily/weekly routine and assess your commitment to self-care. Are you exercising regularly, prioritizing sleep, and building margin into your schedule?
- Ask for the resources you need.
- Seek clarity on your individual role and responsibilities as well as the overall purpose and objective of the team.

Questions for Reflection

- How can I add value to the team in a new way?
- What should I do before our next team meeting that will help the team move forward?
- How am I currently doing in self-care?
- Where can I take initiative without being asked?
- Do I need clarity on my role and the purpose of this team? If so, what am I waiting for?

A Word to Leaders

As a leader, you can play an important role in helping those you lead own their role on the team. It starts with ensuring your team members' roles are well defined, which enables them to clearly see how they can add the most value. It is also important to help team members connect their individual role to the larger purpose of the team.

Next, as you lay out team objectives, be sure to build in adequate time for team members to prepare. It will be difficult for your team to show up well equipped if you as the leader make a habit of last-minute requests and directives. This can be as simple as an email to the team saying, "During our next meeting, we will be discussing the following questions. Please set aside time over the next few days to gather any thoughts you have on this topic so our discussion can be fruitful."

✳ Finally, affirm team members who take initiative (even when they perhaps overstep!). If members of your team are not taking initiative, it could be because you as the leader have created an environment in which team members are afraid to step out of bounds or make mistakes. Affirming initiative, regardless of the outcome, creates a safe environment and gives reluctant team members the confidence they need to stop waiting and start acting.

Chapter Four

Self-Awareness

In my mid-twenties, I (Rusty) went to work as a guide at a guest ranch in Colorado. I led guests on mountain bike trips, backcountry skiing tours, and horseback rides. It was a dream job for a young adventurous twenty-something! It also turned out to be the place I got my first real opportunity to lead a team. One summer, I was given the chance to serve as head wrangler leading a team of about ten staff. A month or two in, I began to feel like the team was in a rut, and I wanted to do something to help. So I crafted a grand plan. On my day off, I went to town and bought a box of donuts from the grocery store, brought it back, and left it in the break room with a note thanking the staff for their work.

Okay, not such a grand plan, but I was sure it would do the trick. When I came back later that afternoon, I noticed the box was still half full, and I did not sense the boost in excitement and morale I had expected. Feeling a bit deflated, I asked the team why they did not seem more encouraged. Their response went something like this: "You've been on our case all summer about every little thing and suddenly you bring donuts, say 'thank you,' and expect everything to be better? It doesn't work that way." Ouch.

I knew I held the staff to a high standard, but I did not realize I was so hard on them. In that moment it became clear I lacked the trust and respect of the team, and my weak attempt at encouragement was not going to overcome a month and a half of overly critical behavior. My staff didn't need donuts; they needed more encouraging leadership.

I wish I had recognized sooner that I was losing the staff's respect and not serving them well. By the time I became aware, it was nearly too late; much of my window to lead effectively that summer was gone. It was a pivotal moment for me, and one that highlights the importance of another critical component of serving others well—self-awareness. And though I happened to be in a leadership role at the time this story took place, the lesson is just as relevant to any member of a team.

Self-awareness is about understanding the way you think, feel, and act and knowing how that impacts others. Steve Moore, author and developer of the Identity Profile Self-Awareness Tool (IPSAT), defines self-awareness as "being honest with yourself, about yourself, and being honest about yourself with others." What a great way to put it.

We are all self-aware to some extent. From the time we are young we learn about ourselves and gain awareness of how others perceive us. When your friends laugh at your jokes, you learn you are funny; when you make varsity, you realize you are athletic; when you are picked last for every sport, you get the hint that you might not be going pro; when you get raving feedback on a presentation, you begin to see a strength in public speaking; and the list goes on.

But self-awareness is not something you fully have or fully lack; it exists on a continuum, and there is always opportunity to deepen or broaden your understanding. As your level of self-awareness increases, so does your ability to interact well with others and perform at your best. Developing self-awareness enables you to create more value and to better serve your team.

One benefit of increased self-awareness is more clarity regarding both your strengths and your weaknesses, which allows you to apply your time and effort in the most helpful ways. Being able to clearly articulate what brings out your best and worst helps you decide which projects to claim, which roles and responsibilities to request, and which opportunities to turn down. It might be tempting to allocate your time and effort to the things you enjoy the most, but don't confuse interest with aptitude—enjoying something does not necessarily mean you are good at it. You owe it to yourself, and your team, to seek the truth about the areas in which you are truly most capable.

Becoming more self-aware also helps you know what and when to hold back. Your team doesn't need all of you, all the time. At WinShape Teams, one of our core values is authenticity. We want our team members to let their behavior unapologetically reflect the attitudes and beliefs shaping it. We don't want people to hide behind a mask. But there is another dimension to this. Part of serving your team is recognizing that not everything you are naturally inclined to do is good and helpful. Telling jokes and injecting humor may be a big part of your personality, and it may bring needed levity to the team, but there are times when it is not beneficial. As for me, I am an external processer and inclined to verbalize to the group everything I am thinking. I have learned over time that it is not always helpful to share every thought in my mind, and it is not inauthentic to exercise restraint.

A third way self-awareness makes you a more effective teammate is by opening your eyes to blind spots—things others know about you but you do not know about yourself. Blind spots can cause all sorts of difficulty in team environments. Maybe there is a team member who dominates every conversation. When he starts talking, everyone in the group knows they are in for a speech, but the dominant talker is oblivious. Or perhaps there is a member of the team who is prone to giving advice. She thinks her counsel is helpful, but others view it as an overreach.

In my donut example above, my team saw me as overly critical and challenging, without a balance of affirmation and encouragement, but I was blind to the way I came across. Whatever the case may be, blind spots create friction, and friction is a barrier to momentum. Seeking to become aware of blind spots can be scary; what you learn can be a bit hurtful. But not knowing something doesn't mean it isn't there, and when you know, you can do something about it.

As you begin to think about your own level of self-awareness, a tool that may be helpful is the Johari Window. Developed in the 1950s by psychologists Joseph Luft and Harry Ingham and further explored in Luft's book *Of Human Interaction*, the model divides our level of awareness regarding behavior, feelings, and motivations into four quadrants.[3]

Quadrant 1 – Known to self and others
Quadrant 2 – Known to others, but not known to self
Quadrant 3 – Known to self, but not known to others
Quadrant 4 – Not known to self or others

	Known to Self	Not Known to Self
Known to Others	*Quadrant 1* Open	*Quadrant 2* Blind
Not Known to Others	*Quadrant 3* Hidden	*Quadrant 4* Unknown

The Johari Window makes it easier to visualize the fact that we all have blind spots, things we keep hidden, and unknown areas yet to be discovered. And the things in each quadrant depend largely on the person or group with whom we are interacting. The bigger the blind, hidden, and unknown quadrants are in any relationship, the fewer things there are in the open, where the most effective interactions can take place. Pursuing increased self-awareness shines a light on blind spots, helps us discover the unknown, and enables us to manage the "hidden" quadrant so that we can better discern what and when to share with others. It brings the appropriate things into the open where they can be most helpful.

Increasing your self-awareness is a great way to serve others, but it is also a great way to find more personal fulfillment. It is much more enjoyable to spend time doing things you are good at than it is to work all day at tasks or projects well outside your gifting and interests. Likewise, when your behavior is off-putting to others and you don't know it, those interactions will be strained, and you are less likely to develop meaningful relationships. As you learn more about yourself and apply that learning to your work with the team, interactions become smoother, and you will enjoy yourself more along the way.

So, what's next? Consider the following suggestions to help you along the journey of self-awareness.

Make the Time

Becoming more self-aware is largely an introspective endeavor. It is about honesty. It is about seeking clarity and committing to gaining a more complete understanding of yourself. This kind of work takes time, but self-reflection is often the first thing to go when life gets busy. Think about your average day. Meeting invitations, kids' sports practice, conference calls, sales meetings, seeing patients, a shift in the warehouse, running the cash register, reviewing profit and loss statements. If you don't prioritize time to reflect, learn, and pursue awareness, it won't happen. You may get feedback on the fly or reflect on your behavior during the commute home, but these informal moments only produce incremental gains, not the type of clarity that will help you contribute at your highest level.

For some, the barrier to self-awareness may not be time but motivation. Perhaps you are confident in the way you act and engage others and don't see a need to learn more about yourself, much less use what you learn to adapt to your surroundings. If that is the case, remember your perspective on your own self-awareness may not necessarily be accurate. We all have blind spots. Think of all the people on your team and assume they all think the same way. Does anyone come to mind who you think could use a little self-awareness? Probably, and chances are you could too.

Take Assessments

Assessments are a wonderful tool for learning about yourself. Assessments provide you with reports, and reports give you information. You can use this information to find resonant words and themes that uniquely describe you. Assessments are a tool, not an authoritative evaluation; they describe you, but they do not define you. Assessments equip you to have a conversation with yourself and with others about how you are wired and how your wiring influences the way you think, feel, and behave. Here are a few additional thoughts to help you get the most value from this type of resource.

- *Don't stop with one.* There are many different types (behavioral, personality, strengths-based), and it is helpful to take a variety. This gives you multiple perspectives to consider.

- *Put them to use.* It is easy to take an assessment, glance at the report, and then put it in a folder and never look at it again. Guilty anyone? This is a waste of time and money. If you go to the trouble of taking it, put in the effort to use what you learn.

- *Involve the whole team.* Learning more about yourself is great, but when the whole team takes an assessment at the same time, it provides an excellent starting point for conversation. Assessments provide a common language that helps team members engage in discussion more easily.

- *Enlist the help of a facilitator.* For most assessments, you can find professionals who are trained to facilitate discussion around the information provided. A well-equipped guide can help you understand the report, process what you learn, and make an action plan.

Seek the Input of Others

None of us will ever be able to uncover all our blind spots without help. Other people can view your life from a different vantage point, and you need more than one perspective.

- ▸ *Solicit feedback.* This topic is addressed in more depth later in the book, but it is worth mentioning briefly here. When was the last time you asked someone for feedback and receptively listened to what they had to say? Make a habit of sitting with peers, supervisors, and direct reports to ask what you are doing well and what you could do that would be helpful for them. A formal tool, such as a 360-degree assessment, is also a great resource, particularly if you want to see what themes emerge in the feedback of others.

- ▸ *Hire a coach.* At first, it may seem odd to think about paying someone as a life or business coach. But what is so odd about asking someone to help you be the best version of yourself? I worked with a personal coach for two years, and it was immensely valuable. One conversation in particular stands out as a watershed moment. As we were discussing my personal progress over the previous year, I had to confront the fact that I was neglecting several key areas of my life, areas I claimed were important priorities. As I came to this realization, my coach challenged me by saying, "At some point, you must ask yourself if you are a fraud or if you really believe what you say you believe." His words hit me hard, and I had to ask some tough questions. As a result, I made some changes in life that have been incredibly impactful. I needed his perspective to help me see what I couldn't.

Initiate Action ✳

The true value of self-awareness comes from applying what you learn; the information becomes useful when you put it into practice. Action is the critical but often neglected step. Once you begin to learn more about yourself, here are a few ways you can put your newfound revelation to work.

- *Consolidate your learnings.* Assessments, feedback, coaching, and personal reflection can produce a lot of information, which can be overwhelming. It is helpful to identify themes and pull a few takeaways on which to focus.
- *Practice.* If you learn people feel you are removed and unapproachable, schedule small blocks of time to walk around the office and just check in with others. Literally put appointments on your calendar titled "walk around the office." If you discover you come across as curt and direct, make it a point to ask about someone's day before making a request. It may feel unnatural (because for you it is), but all new things feel awkward at first.
- *Follow up.* If you receive feedback or discover a blind spot and then alter your behavior accordingly, follow up with others to see if the action you are taking has been helpful. Then, adjust as needed.

Closing Thought

One benefit of increased self-awareness is more clarity regarding both your strengths and your weaknesses, which allows you to apply your time and effort in the most helpful ways. Being able to clearly articulate what brings out your best and worst helps you decide which projects to claim, which roles and responsibilities to request, and which opportunities to turn down. Pursuing increased self-awareness shines a light on blind spots, helps us discover the unknown, and enables us to manage the "hidden" quadrant so that we can better discern what and when to share with others. As you learn more about yourself and apply that learning to your work with the team, interaction becomes smoother, and you will enjoy yourself more along the way.

Questions for Reflection

- ▸ Am I motivated to build self-awareness? If not, why not?
- ▸ What are my strengths and weaknesses as a team member, and how do they impact my role on the team? Where can I be more engaged, and where should I be more restrained?
- ▸ How do other members of my team view me? What do they see as my strengths and weaknesses, and how does their assessment differ from my own?
- ▸ Where can I make time to learn more about myself through introspection and feedback?
- ▸ What concrete steps can I take to put self-assessment into action?

A Word to Leaders

As a leader, you can help your staff in this area. Here are two specific suggestions.

First, provide consistent, specific feedback. Observe your reports in meetings, pay attention to their interactions with you and with others, notice the things they do well and the situations in which they struggle. Then share your observations with them in a caring and constructive way.

Second, commit resources and funding to your staff's pursuit of greater awareness. Purchase an assessment for an individual or the whole team, and hire someone to facilitate the processing. Set aside dollars for team member coaching, and help find someone who is a good fit. Allow for margin in staff schedules so there is time to reflect and learn. The way in which you allocate resources sends a message about what is important to you.

Finally, as you help your team members become more aware, don't forget to increase your own level of self-awareness. Otherwise, you will have a donut story of your own to tell for years to come.

- possibly view me as too harsh, maybe even scary. but also can be fun. not ~~scary wilder~~ i feel as though i view myself the same way, but i justify my weaknesses.

- taking more INTENTIONAL time to reflect, looking at the parts of me that can be intense.

- journaling, implementing more ways of recieving feedback

Chapter Five

Creating Clarity

You can learn a lot about teamsmanship from the process of making a peanut butter and jelly sandwich. There is an exercise we do with clients in which a group of people provides the facilitator with step-by-step instructions for how to make a PB & J, as though he or she had never made one. The facilitator stands at a table supplied with all the necessary ingredients, and each participant provides instructions for one step of the process. The exercise is over when the sandwich is fully assembled. Easy, right?

Well, here is a sample of some common instructions, and the facilitator's response. A participant says "open the bread," and the facilitator picks up the loaf and tears the plastic apart. Someone says "spread some peanut butter on the bread," and the facilitator puts his or her hand in the peanut butter, grabs a glob, and spreads it on the bread. Toward the end, someone usually says, "now, put the two pieces of bread together." The facilitator picks up the pieces and puts them together with the peanut butter and jelly facing the outside. You get the idea. Many of the instructions lack the specificity needed to be effective, and the facilitator's action does not match the participant's intent; there is a lack of clarity.

The exercise is usually funny to watch. It is designed to be amusing, but it does a good job of illustrating the difficulties resulting from unclear communication. Without clarity, there is confusion and frustration. People waste time and effort doing the wrong things. You can probably recall plenty of real-life situations in which a lack of clarity created real challenges for you and your team.

Maybe a boss gave you an assignment, you executed, and then you realized he or she had something very different in mind. Maybe you had a conversation with a coworker and later discovered your perspective was misunderstood. Perhaps you found yourself operating with little or no information, having to guess what others were expecting and hoping things would turn out well. Or perhaps the example that comes to mind is a time when your own efforts at clear communication fell short. Whatever the specifics, the absence of clarity makes things harder, and its absence is a common reality for teams.

One of the reasons clarity is so often lacking is each team member believes its absence is someone else's fault and therefore someone else's responsibility to fix. More time is often spent talking about the need for clarity than working on creating it. There is a big difference between wishing things were different and working to make them better, and servant team members always take the latter approach. Instead of saying, "If only *someone else* would," servant team members ask themselves, "What can *I* do to help?" or "What can I do to help others better understand my intent?" or "What can I do to get the information

I need?" or "What can I do to limit the assumptions I make when others are communicating?"

Asking these questions puts you in a position to be part of the solution, moving the team forward. If clarity is the goal, assigning blame or waiting for someone else to step up won't help. What the team needs is for each team member to move beyond wanting clarity to committing to create clarity. Specifically, this means actively seeking clarity from, and providing clarity to, both the leader and the other members of the team.

Seek Clarity

Creating clarity starts with seeking clarity from others, and that means taking initiative. Don't wait for clarity; go get it. It is easy to point fingers at the leader or project manager. That approach often goes something like this: "If only he or she would give direction, we would know what to do. In the meantime, we will just wait and be confused and frustrated." It may sound a bit ridiculous when you say it that way, but it happens all the time. This type of thinking is much more self-centered than team focused.

Waiting for clarity that may never come is not an effective means of helping your team be successful. Sure, it would be great if every leader made things crystal clear for the teams they lead, but this is not the reality. Even the best leaders will never prevent all confusion and ambiguity for everyone, so team members must decide how to respond to the ambiguity that will certainly come. Instead of blaming or settling in frustration, choose to be part of the solution. When you don't know something, ask. If you are unsure about your role or what is expected, reach out and pursue the clarity you need. If no one knows the answer, help create it. Propose an idea, help shape the expectations, and then help communicate with others.

✳ In addition to initiative, seeking clarity also requires humility. Our pride can be an ugly thing, and if we let it, it will stand in the way of high performance. It can be hard to admit we don't understand something. There is fear that asking questions will make us look unintelligent or unprepared, so we press on in the dark, hoping we will figure things out as we go.

However, there is a cost to walking in the dark—it takes longer, you have to feel your way around, and you may not get where you are trying to go. It may be embarrassing to admit you need clarity, but it's much better to get the information you need than to create workarounds, put off important decisions, or risk making mistakes just to avoid looking bad. Our pride also affects our desire to seek clarity when we believe someone else has fallen short in their communication. Pride can lead us to think, "It's not my job to make up for someone else's poor communication." But again, this is not a helpful attitude. Serving your team well requires the humility to put those feelings aside and seek the clarity you need to be successful.

Provide Clarity

Just as important as seeking clarity from others is an intentional focus on providing clarity to others. When we speak or write, we assume we will be understood, believing that telling others what we want them to know automatically means we have clearly communicated. But telling and communicating are not the same thing, and we mustn't confuse words spoken with clarity provided.

I think the peanut butter and jelly exercise demonstrates this well. To the one giving instructions, knowing to put the peanut butter and jelly on the *inside* when putting the bread together is assumed, but this is obviously not clear to someone who has never made a sandwich. The same is true in all aspects of life. Everyone on the team has a different personality, different life experiences, different priorities, and a different style of communicating. What seems clear to one person may not be clear to another. Providing clarity means adjusting the way you communicate for the benefit of those around you.

Another imperative for those seeking to provide clarity is having grace for others with whom you are communicating. If you feel like you have communicated your thoughts well, it can be tempting to shut others down when they ask questions. "I've done my part," we think, now it is up to others to act accordingly. Responses like, "I put that in the email last week, so you should know" or "I covered that in our first meeting" close the conversation abruptly and make it less likely teammates will seek the clarity they need. If the goal is effective communication, trying to prove you have already provided the necessary information is counterproductive to the objective. Taking a gracious approach keeps the lines of communication open and creates a safe environment to ask questions.

Think about your current team at work or in any other sphere of life. If everyone took the initiative to humbly seek the clarity they need rather than waiting for someone else to act, what effect might that have? If everyone intentionally focused on graciously providing clarity, not simply assuming they are understood, how could that improve the performance of the team and the fulfillment of its members? As you seek to help your team in this way, consider the following two actions that can help you do it well: doing your homework and asking questions.

Do Your Homework

Before you can ask others for clarity or provide clarity to others, you must first be able to clearly articulate for yourself what it is you need to know or want to communicate. Here are three ways you can prepare before engaging others.

- *Get specific about what you need.* The general statement "I need clarity" is not particularly helpful, though I certainly understand the feeling. It is a bit like saying "I don't like it" when you give feedback on a project. It indicates there is a problem, but it doesn't provide much direction on how to find a solution. Instead of saying, "I need clarity," do a little prework to gather your thoughts. What are one or two things that are unclear specifically? From whom do you need information? What information would be most helpful to you right now? Once you know what you need, it will be much easier for others to help.
- *Prepare talking points.* When we get busy, we often run from one thing to the next without taking time to prepare. This can cause us to make a habit of "winging it" in meetings or conversations with others and that can affect our ability to provide clarity. If you have something important to communicate, take time on the front end to think through the points you want to make.
- *Know your audience.* It is easy to fall into a rhythm of communicating in the way most natural or comfortable for you. And, while this is not wrong, it will be easier for others to receive what you are communicating if you provide the information in the way most helpful to them. Invest in learning the communication styles and preferences of the others on your team. Do they prefer written

or verbal communication? Does it need to be one on one, or can the information be delivered in a group setting? Sometimes creating clarity requires a step outside of your comfort zone for the good of the team.

Ask Questions

Questions are the key to clarity. In my experience, asking more questions is the one adjustment that can make the biggest difference in your ability to communicate effectively, and this affects both seeking and providing clarity. When seeking clarity, use questions to learn more. When providing clarity, use questions to discover gaps and check for understanding.

- ▸ *Questions to learn.* When we communicate, we can become so focused on responding that we neglect to ensure we really understand the other person's point of view. As a result, a lot of words are exchanged but no effective communication takes place. Before responding, ask questions to draw out more information. Questions like, "Would you tell me more about that?" or "Would you be willing to unpack that last statement for me?" demonstrate a genuine desire to understand and prevent the frustrating back-and-forth that occurs when two people are primarily focused on telling the other person what is on their mind.

- ▸ *Questions to discover gaps.* I am an explainer. Some might say an overexplainer. Okay, most would say I chronically overexplain. The good thing about explanations is they can provide helpful information that brings clarity. But if our explanations do not address the information people need most, they become unnecessary noise drowning out the main message and making things less clear. Questions are a great way to discover the gaps in someone else's understanding, which then allows you to provide the information most needed by the person with whom you are engaging. As simple as it sounds, the best way to find out what information people need most is to ask them, a step we too often ignore.

▸ Questions to check for understanding. This gets back to the basics of communication. After providing information, ask, "What did you hear me say?" and after receiving information, say, "What I heard you say was [fill in the blank], is that correct?" While this approach can seem a bit awkward or stilted, it is a great way to catch miscommunication early and create clarity in the team.

Closing Thought

Creating clarity starts with seeking clarity from others, and that means taking initiative. Don't wait for clarity; go get it. When you don't know something, ask. If you are unsure about your role or what is expected, reach out and pursue the clarity you need. If no one knows the answer, help create it. Providing clarity means adjusting the way you communicate for the benefit of those around you. Remember, the goal is effective communication, not proving you're right.

Questions for Reflection

▸ What do you need clarity on right now? Who could provide it?

- ▸ Where is your pride preventing you from seeking the clarity you need?
- ▸ Who currently needs clarity from you? On what?
- ▸ Where do you need to gain clarity for yourself so you can provide it to others?

A Word to Leaders

As discussed above, it is everyone on the team's responsibility to provide and seek clarity, but you as the leader bear the largest responsibility for clearly communicating roles, responsibilities, and expectations. If you haven't shared your expectations with the team, they probably don't know what they are. Does everyone on your team have a job description? Does each person know his or her specific role in each project? There are few more helpful things you can do as a leader than ensuring everyone knows where the team is going and who is responsible for what to get you there.

If your team is lacking clarity, it may not be a communication problem; it could be because you don't know what your expectations are. You as the leader need to do your homework too. There is a saying: "If there is mist in the pulpit, there will be fog in the pews." Things can't be clear for your team if they are not clear for you, so it is essential you set aside time to formulate your thoughts and expectations before asking the team to act. No one expects you to have all the answers, but don't send the team to wander in the woods while you sit back at camp trying to decide where you want to go.

Chapter Six

Maintaining Perspective

In the summer of 2013, I (Rusty) set out with a group of friends to climb Grand Teton, a 13,775-foot peak in Jackson, Wyoming. The closer we got to the top, the smaller and more exposed I felt in comparison to the immensity of the mountain we were climbing. I felt insignificant and vulnerable. It was as though I was in another world entirely and the trailhead below seemed a million miles away.

But perhaps Grand Teton is not so big after all. In 1972, the crew of Apollo 17 captured what has become an iconic image. Known as *Blue Marble*, the image shows a perfect view of Earth from space. Almost the entire continent of Africa can be seen along with oceans, clouds, and the Arabian Peninsula. When I look at that image, with all of Earth captured in one frame, it puts the size of a mountain like Grand Teton into a new context.

But then why stop with Earth? In 1990, Hubble Space Telescope was launched into orbit to capture images of space from outside Earth's atmosphere. Hubble has taken many magnificent photos over the years, but perhaps the most awe inspiring is called *Hubble Ultra Deep Field*. This lone image, requiring eight hundred exposures to capture, contains nearly ten thousand galaxies—ten thousand!—spanning billions of light years. It is a deep look into a tiny section of the sky that reveals the seemingly infinite scope of our universe. So Earth, in all its grandeur, is not so large after all. It is but one planet, in one solar system, in one galaxy, in a universe so large almost ten thousand galaxies can be captured in a single image.

The lesson here is not that Grand Teton is small or that Earth is insignificant. Rather, the point of this example is to bring to life the universal truth that our perception of reality is largely dependent on our *perspective*. And this relates not only to how we see physical objects but to how we perceive everything we face in life. Whether it be a physical mountain or a challenge at work, the size and importance of the things before us is relative, not fixed, and our ability to recognize this, and keep things in proper perspective, has a dramatic impact on our fulfillment and productivity, both as individuals and as teams.

When we fail to keep things in perspective, the size and significance of every task, challenge, setback, and concern becomes distorted and appears larger than it is. We are inclined to assess reality based on that which is directly before us, forgetting that proximity and the vantage point from which we are looking have a dramatic effect on our perception. Without an accurate assessment of the landscape ahead, things that are ordinary bumps in the road become in our minds mountains to be climbed. This causes us to invest far too much time, energy, effort, and emotional bandwidth on relatively unimportant things.

When everything looks big, everything requires attention, and it can quickly seem as though there is more to do than can ever be accomplished. We can easily become overwhelmed, frustrated, and stuck as we shoulder the weight of a burden that need not exist. Perhaps you can relate.

The challenges of losing perspective also carry over from the individual to the team, causing the team to get bogged down in relatively minor issues. I recall a leadership team meeting during which I raised a question about a clothing item we gave to each member of our staff. I felt the timing and expense of the purchase might have been unwise and raised my concern to the team. As these things go, the conversation moved from the wisdom of that purchase to our entire approach to staff care.

Our interpersonal dynamic took a hit, and we spent more time than I am willing to admit circling around the issue. Keep in mind this was a leadership team meeting, and I am quite certain we had more important things to spend our limited time on than what sweatshirts we should buy our staff. The question was not entirely problematic, but there was no need for such a small ember to be fanned into the campfire it became.

The encouraging news is perspective can be gained as readily as it can be lost, and you can leverage proper perspective to help your team be better. By intentionally grounding your outlook in what is real and what is true rather than what you see in the moment, you can accurately assess the relative size and importance of the things you face. Then you can steer your own efforts, and the efforts of your team, toward the things truly of highest importance.

✳ Having proper perspective better equips you to be selective in the concerns you bring to the team rather than sharing everything on your mind. It enables you to discern the difference between a significant challenge and a minor setback and manage your response accordingly. With proper perspective, you can help your team move forward; without it, chances are high you will hold your team back.

So how does one go about gaining and maintaining perspective? As we have said before, our beliefs are the root of our behaviors, so it begins with acknowledging your perspective is incomplete. If you don't believe your perspective is limited, there is no reason to work toward a new reality, so this is a critical first step. At some point, you have probably seen the phrase "objects in mirror are closer than they appear" on the passenger side-view mirror of a car. It warns the driver that what he or she sees in the mirror is a slightly distorted view of what is happening. Without this warning, drivers wouldn't know the image was distorted. They would make decisions based on incorrect information, which could lead to an accident. The warning helps the driver adjust his or her behavior to match reality rather than perception.

Just as there is a gap between what the driver sees and what is really there, there is often a gap between what we perceive and what is true in our team environments. Unfortunately, however, unlike the passenger side mirror, most things in life do not come with a warning making clear the limitations of our point of view. Absent this warning, we take our perception to be reality, which can lead to "accidents" in our lives and in our teams. Acknowledging our perception is not objectively true allows us to take steps toward gaining a clearer and more complete outlook—things like stepping back, slowing down, and digging deeper.

Step Back

Perhaps the primary barrier to maintaining perspective is letting our world get too small. Our proximity to the challenges, difficulties, and even the opportunities before us distorts their perceived size and importance. It might be letting a small problem hijack an entire meeting, allowing a minor personal offense to derail a relationship, spending entirely too much time and energy fine-tuning a relatively small project, or wasting precious time with loved ones by ruminating on the day's frustrations rather than engaging in the moment.

Or it could be any one of countless other ways we magnify challenges, issues, and setbacks so they seem much larger than they really are. The closer we are to something, the larger it appears, so a great way to gain perspective is to simply step back and increase your field of vision. Stepping back helps to answer the question, "In the grand scheme of things, how important is the issue or challenge before me/us?" Much like viewing Grand Teton from space changes its perceived size, viewing our work from a new vantage point helps us gain clarity on its importance relative to everything else on the list.

There are many ways to put space between you and whatever you are facing, and the approach you take should largely be driven by the amount of distance needed. Sometimes all you need is something quick.

- *Step away from the computer and take a quick walk.* In our office we have a nine iron and a pile of golf balls; they get put to good use.
- *Briefly excuse yourself from a meeting or ask the whole team for a ten-minute break.* When momentum builds in a meeting, it takes on a life of its own. Everyone layers their thoughts one on top of the other until you barely know where you started. A break is often much more productive than saying one more thing.

▸ *Get a good night's sleep.* Before you send that email, confront a coworker, or stare at the same paragraph for another two hours, sleep on it. I have found sleep to have a seemingly magical power to put things back into proper perspective.

Other times, regaining perspective may require you to zoom out further.

▸ *Set "it"—whatever "it" is—aside for a while.* Ironically, while writing this chapter on perspective, I found myself getting stuck. What helped the most was setting it aside, moving on to other things, and then coming back with fresh thoughts.

▸ *Work in a new environment.* New surroundings can often bring a change in perspective.

▸ *Get away.* When I was fifteen years old, I traveled to Africa for the first time on a medical relief trip. Since that trip, I have had the privilege of visiting many countries, and I always find travel to bring new and needed perspective. Whether it is a visit to another country, a weekend getaway, or just a change in everyday environment, find an opportunity to expand your world. This is not always easy or practical, but it is huge. Don't underestimate the life-changing impact of a well-timed getaway, particularly to a place radically different from your normal world.

Slow Down

Pace and perspective are directly related. Moving too fast inclines us to focus only on what is directly ahead rather than considering how that which feels most pressing relates to everything else. This can easily cause us to misjudge the relative importance of the next thing without even realizing we are doing so. Gaining perspective is often a reflective process, and reflection is very difficult when there is no margin.

Slowing down creates space to think and prioritize, enabling you to put your best effort toward the most important things and help your team do the same. Both your time and your team's time are finite, and there will never be enough of either to do or discuss everything that comes up. Getting a lot done is only helpful if you do the right things and do them in a healthy way. So, while it is tempting to speed up or cram more in, maintaining perspective requires you to set a sustainable pace.

This can be challenging in a world that seems addicted to busyness, but a few simple, practical actions can make a big difference.

- *Build in a minimum of fifteen minutes between meetings.* This allows you time to reflect on what just happened and prepare for what is ahead.
- *Schedule blocks on your calendar to think and process.* Try setting aside the last thirty minutes of every day and at least one day a month to look back and look ahead.
- *Put less on your meeting agenda.* I have been to many more meetings that ran long than finished early, and I expect that is common. An overloaded agenda makes things feel rushed, and when we feel rushed things tend to escalate.
- *Schedule your meeting times to be shorter than normal.* If you regularly meet for one hour, schedule the time to be fifty minutes. If a quick check-in with a team member

is thirty minutes, set the time on your calendar for twenty-five minutes. We will fill whatever time we have on the calendar, so use the calendar to your advantage.

Dig Deeper

Given the limitations of our perspective, we are foolish not to recognize the value of multiple points of view. Whether you are making much of something relatively small or missing important information that would provide a more complete understanding, digging deeper to see other perspectives is essential. The main way to accomplish this is to ask questions of others. We all have blind spots, and others are often uniquely positioned to see things obscuring our view. The following suggestions can help you dig deeper to find a more complete perspective.

- *Identify what feels off.* Most of the time we can sense when our perspective is off. We don't feel at ease. We can't get the topic off our mind. It feels contentious every time we bring it up with the team. Be aware of what is going on in your head and around you. Be honest about your need for more information.
- *Build diversity.* Invite input from people who don't look like you, think like you, or share your same experience. Talk to people with whom you often disagree. Otherwise, you are just confirming what you already believe.
- *Ask those you trust.* Diversity is essential, but so is input from those who know you well. We all have blind spots, and trusted advisors can help you find them. Reach out to a teammate you trust and ask them what they see.

- *Look back to similar situations.* If you pause and reflect, you have probably faced a similar situation in the past. What did you learn from it? What appears to be the same as before? What appears to be different? Don't forget to draw from previous experience to help you in the future.

Closing Thought

When we fail to keep things in perspective, the size and significance of every task, challenge, setback, and concern becomes distorted and appears larger than it is. When everything looks big, everything requires attention, and it can quickly seem as though there is more to do than can ever be accomplished. Thankfully, perspective can be gained as readily as it can be lost, and you can leverage proper perspective to help your team be better. The closer we are to something, the larger it appears, so a great way to gain perspective is to simply step back and increase your field of vision.

Questions for Reflection

- Does your behavior indicate that you realize the limitations of your perspective?
- Who is a trusted resource whom you can trust to help you maintain perspective?
- What is something to which you are currently too close? What step can you take to pull back and regain perspective?
- What rhythms do you have in place to help you maintain perspective? What could you start doing regularly to help?

A Word to Leaders

Leaders, your actions and words often carry additional weight. Keeping things in perspective helps you keep the team on track. Likewise, when you lose perspective, you are likely to hold up the entire team. Remind yourself and your team that perspective is not often permanent. Even when you've clarified your thinking and refocused your priorities, two or three work-related "molehills" in a row can easily distort your frame of reference. When you sense your team or one of its members is losing perspective, challenge them to apply the best practices described above. You are well positioned to see things from a higher altitude and to help your team determine the relative size of the challenges they face and the blind spots and limitations of their perspectives.

Team meetings are also a critical environment in which you can help the team focus its time and energy on the most important priorities. Team members will naturally be close to their individual areas of focus, so you can add unique value by keeping the broader landscape in view. However, remember, no one, not even the team leader, has a complete perspective, so resist the temptation to believe your position of leadership comes with an unlimited field of vision.

Chapter Seven

Responding to Change

On April 12, 1945, Franklin D. Roosevelt died in the first year of his fourth term as president of the United States. At the time of his death, Roosevelt had been president for more than twelve years, and as biographer David McCullough observed, "He had been President for so long and through such trying, stirring times that it seemed to many Americans...that he was virtually the presidency itself."[4] Roosevelt's death meant Harry Truman, a former US senator from Missouri and the newly elected vice president, was abruptly thrust into the highest office in the country.

Unlike Roosevelt, who had many years of experience in the executive branch, Truman had only been vice president for three months when he unexpectedly took the oath of office. The United States was fighting World War II, and there was no shortage of life-altering decisions to be made. The day after he was sworn in, the new president petitioned a group of reporters, saying, "Boys, if you ever pray, pray for me now. I don't know whether you fellows ever had a load of hay fall on you, but when they told me yesterday what had happened, I felt like the moon, the stars, and all the planets had fallen on me."[5] With no runway and very little preparation for all he would face, Harry Truman became the president of the United States, and he was acutely aware it was an enormous responsibility.

There is no doubt what Truman experienced was a significant change. His life was set on a new course, and he felt in the moment as if the sky had fallen on him. Like Truman, many of us know the feeling of being burdened by the weight of an uncertain future and a new reality. We may not find ourselves leading a country anytime soon, but every team member will most certainly face change, and even small deviations from our expectations or norm can feel hard and overwhelming. Unless you are the initiator, change has the tendency to make you feel out of control. It can mean additional work or the loss of something you enjoyed or found useful. It can mean a disruption in your usual schedule.

Change can be disruptive, uncomfortable, and it can put you and your team on a path you would not necessarily have chosen.

Change for a team can come in a variety of forms. A team member may be added or a key system or process may be altered without your input. Perhaps your team will be given a new project with little notice, the team will get a new leader, or one of your peers might suggest an idea or solution that will lead the team in a vastly different direction.

Oftentimes one change will have a ripple effect, impacting multiple teams. Last year, in our organization, we made a structural adjustment that meant moving an entire department out of our division. That impacted the makeup of our leadership team, our culture, and our process for doing work, among other things. Change is inevitable, and it is necessary, but it can also be hard. How a team and its members manage change is a critical factor in team performance and health. For this reason, times of change are great opportunities for you to create real value for your team by making sure all your efforts move the team toward a better future, rather than holding the team back. This means responding rather than reacting and working to ensure the best possible result.

Respond vs. React

When you first learn of a change, you have the option of choosing either to respond or react, and there is a big difference between the two. Experiencing change or even discussing a proposed change can cause us to feel everything from fear and anxiety to sadness and frustration, and everything in between.

Reactions are the unprocessed and unbridled expression of these emotions. They are vocal or behavioral manifestations of our initial feelings about something. Reactions are reflexive, like your leg kicking forward when a doctor taps your knee with a mallet. Reacting puts the focus on you and derails the team's efforts to move forward. It makes things tenser and more difficult.

Responses on the other hand are more measured. You experience the same emotions, but instead of simply reacting, you process what you are feeling and choose what to say or do next. Responses are thoughtful and considered. When we react to something, we may blurt out the first thing we think or feel, but responding requires self-control. It is not about suppressing emotion but rather managing our emotions for the good of the team. It is the difference between saying, "That's ridiculous. Why do we have to use this new system? They are always changing things!" and "I've got concerns about using this new system. It will mean some significant changes for me, and I've got some questions about how that will work."

The same fear may be driving both statements, but they have a very different effect on the team. Responding puts the focus on making progress and creating solutions—we have new information, a new reality, now what? Responding does not necessarily mean agreeing with a change or neglecting to share concerns. If you believe a change is not best, you should say so, but do so in a constructive way, ensuring your input is focused on being helpful, not simply drawing the team's attention to how the change impacts you.

Much of a team's time is spent discussing potential changes, and your ability to respond rather than react to suggested change can help create a safe environment in the team, which is essential for team health. I remember a conversation I had with my wife, Bekah (yes, a marriage is a team!), that illustrates this point. We had been married about two and a half years when we had our first son, Dawson. We were both working full-time, and Bekah was planning to resume a mostly full-time schedule at the end of her maternity leave.

As her return to work drew nearer, I could sense she was starting to question whether that was the best choice for our family. About two weeks before Bekah was set to start back, I got a call from her as I was driving home. Through tears, she said she didn't think it was best for her to go back; she wanted to change course and stay home with Dawson instead.

I was scared. Neither of us made much money, and Bekah's income was higher than mine, so being a single-income family didn't seem like an option. The fear I felt was pushing me to react with statements like "that can't work" or "we'll never afford it," but thankfully I was able to recognize the importance of the moment and choose to respond instead. Rather than reacting and shutting her down, I tried to be as supportive as I could be and told her we would figure it out; it would be okay.

I hung up the phone having no answers but knowing it was an important decision. She felt strongly about the situation, and I knew we needed to make it work. In talking with her later, I learned my response to her in that moment was very important in helping her feel safe to share her thoughts. Had I reacted out of fear, it would have created tension, shut her down, and could have made her less likely to share her thoughts openly in the future.

This same dynamic is at play in all our teams. When someone proposes a change, a new idea to the team, they are being vulnerable. If members of the team react rather than respond, it can stifle the process, diminish safety, and limit potential.

Responding to change is not something you will get right all the time. But in your efforts to do so, there are several things you can do to help you be more consistent and successful.

- ▸ *Practice good self-care.* The healthier you are as an individual, the more prepared you will be to respond well to change. If you aren't getting enough rest, exercise, or personal restoration, you are more likely to find yourself reacting as opposed to responding. Set goals around things like rest, fitness, morning routine, healthy eating, and designated quiet time.
- ▸ *Request time to process.* We can't control how we feel in the moment, but we can control what we do with those feelings. However, that can be difficult to do in real time. I have found, when I feel a reaction coming, it is helpful

to ask for some time to process before sharing any thoughts. It allows me to step away, consider what I am feeling, and decide what I want to do with that information. When you take time, you can ask yourself, "Why am I feeling this way? Why is this change making me fearful, nervous, unhappy, angry, or upset?" Much better to give yourself space to process those thoughts than to let those emotions drive potentially disruptive behavior in the moment (e.g., shouting, frustrated comments, critical remarks, fear-based disagreement) you may regret later. In a healthy team, both the leader and other members will be comfortable giving each other time to process change and respond rather than react to it.

▸ *Pursue additional information.* Oftentimes what we hear first is a limited version of what is happening. If we immediately react to the first bit of information we receive, we end up expressing our thoughts before we have learned enough to form a considered response. Pursuing additional information helps fill the gaps often left open in the first pass. When news of a change is communicated, it often begins with sharing the "what." Pursuing additional information allows you to discover things like the "why" and the "how" that can paint a more complete picture.

Work to Ensure the Best Possible Result

Regardless of how you feel about a change, once it has been made it is time to become a champion for the best possible outcome. When a change has been made you either didn't want, didn't expect, or perhaps actively advocated against, it is easy to take an unhelpful posture toward the new reality. You may be tempted to point out the problems the change has caused or to make sure the team remembers you were against the change from the start.

I recall a situation in our organization when the decision was made to restructure our sales department, which meant I had less direct influence over that work. There were good reasons for the change, but to me, the cons outweighed the pros. For a period of several years I struggled to support the change, and I'm sure I missed quite a few opportunities to serve the common goal.

When something wasn't working, I trended more toward "if only we would go back to how it was" than "what are some things we could do to overcome that challenge within the current system?" There were times along the way when I leaned in and took helpful steps, but there were also plenty of times when I was content to be frustrated about what wasn't working rather than committing to do everything I could to ensure a good result.

If I'm honest, I'm not sure I really wanted the change to succeed. I had a different idea of what was best and right, and ultimately I wanted that solution to be the outcome. Of course, the truth is the success of my team was directly connected to the success of that change, so anything I did to help would have been in all our common interest. Complaining about a change or separating yourself from it doesn't help the team accomplish its goals any more effectively. It is more important to be helpful than to be right.

Here are two ways to put all your effort toward ensuring change is successful and to minimize potentially negative effects of the change.

1. *Ask how you can help.* Team members who are primarily looking out for themselves react to change by looking for ways to make it easier on them. Instead of looking inwardly, ask what you can do to help ensure the change will bring the best result possible. You may not get to control whether the change occurs, but you may be able to play a significant role in how it impacts the team's performance.

2. *Focus on what will be gained, not what will be lost.* If we focus only on the negative aspects of change, it is easy to paint a bleak picture. It is important to identify and address relevant challenges and implications; blind optimism is rarely helpful. However, resist the temptation to be consumed by this part of the process. Along with change comes the chance to create a new future; this is exciting! When we fix our eyes on this new vision, it is much easier to stay motivated through the bumps in the road.

One important note is there may come a time when your team or your leader will adopt a change you simply cannot support. Championing the change would require something of you that you are not willing or able to give. In this case, you still have the choice between reacting and responding, and you can still serve the team by choosing to respond. It may be the best response is to step away from the team or even exit the organization, depending on the situation. Serving well does not mean moving forward with the team at all costs.

Closing Thought

Reactions are the unprocessed and unbridled expression of emotions. They are vocal or behavioral manifestations of our initial feelings about something. Responses on the other hand are much more measured. You experience the same emotions, but instead of simply reacting, you process what you are feeling and choose what to say or do next. This same dynamic is at play in all our teams. When someone proposes a change, a new idea to the team, they are being vulnerable. If members of the team react rather than respond, it can stifle the process, diminish safety, and limit potential. Responding to change is not something you will get right all the time, but measured responses will almost always lead to healthier handling of team change.

Questions for Reflection

- Do I have more control than I realize?
- Is what I'm feeling/how I'm reacting helpful to the team?
- Is there something I am currently doing that is preventing this change, and this team, from being as successful as it could be?
- What is something I could be doing right now to help this change be successful?
- Am I more focused on being helpful or on being right?

A Word to Leaders

The way in which you lead and communicate change can have a huge impact on the way your team members respond. It is much easier for people to respond productively to change when they have a chance to prepare and be part of the process. Rather than blindsiding your team with changes and then asking for their support, help them be successful by gathering input, giving context when possible, and creating space for team members to process. This is a great reason to get to know your team members personally. If you lead an individual who struggles with change or is more prone to knee-jerk reactions, you may need to inform him or her about change separately or provide information in smaller chunks.

Chapter Eight

Being Trustworthy

For many years, an expected part of team-building programs has been an exercise called the "trust fall." For those of you who have experienced it, it was most likely memorable. For those who haven't, here is the basic idea. One person from the group stands several feet off the ground on an object (often a wooden platform) with his or her back to the rest of the group. The other team members form two lines facing one another and hold their arms out in front of them in an alternating "zipper" pattern. These team members form a receiving line of sorts. The person on the platform stands very stiffly and then, after confirming the group is ready to catch, falls backward off the platform into the outstretched arms of his or her teammates, who then lower the participant carefully back to the ground. The activity is typically done as the culmination of a series of progressively challenging trust-based exercises, beginning with simply leaning back and being "caught" by a partner and ending with the elevated fall into the team's arms.

While this activity has been a staple in the traditional team-building industry, we stopped including it in our programs years ago. We wanted to have a different conversation about trust. Trust doesn't come from activities like falling from a platform and being caught by a team. The fact that someone prevents you from crashing to the ground and getting hurt does not mean trust is present in the relationship. Trust is built over time; it is an outcome.

Without trust there is no safety, no community. In fact, without trust there really is no team at all. If team members do not trust one another, they are not likely to work well together toward a common goal. Perhaps this is the reason trust is one of the most commonly discussed topics when it comes to teams. It is foundational. If trust is not present, or it is lost, there are few things more important than working to build or restore trust in the team.

However, though we often talk about building trust as a team, as in "our team needs to work on trust," that is a bit misleading. The level of trust in a team is only as high as the level of trust existing between the individual members. Trust is not a right to be demanded from others. It is earned through service to them. For you as the team member, that means the best way to build trust in your team is to be trust*worthy*, earning your team's trust each day. Two ways you can do that are through sacrifice and consistency.

Sacrifice

The best teams are made of people who are *for* each other rather than *against* each other, and you can feel the difference. Trust in a relationship is lost when we stop believing someone has our best interest at heart, when we wonder if they are acting only for themselves without considering our interests or the interests of others. However, trust is gained when others value our needs and actively pursue our well-being. Trust is gained through sacrifice.

When you sacrifice for someone, you communicate "you are important to me—so important that I am willing to put aside my own needs to meet yours." And while it is nice to hear someone say they are in your corner, that sentiment comes to life in a new way when they do something for you that was costly to them.

One year, my kids were getting an outdoor play set for Christmas. We wanted it to be a surprise, but a huge play set in the backyard is a bit tricky to keep hidden. So it needed to be built at the last minute, which meant Christmas Eve. Now, if you have ever put together a wooden play set from a kit, you will know it is an exercise in patience, and an extra set of hands can be invaluable.

I put out a request, and one of my coworkers came to my house, on Christmas Eve, and helped me put it together—it took hours! Talk about a sacrifice. A couple of years later, a tree fell on another team member's play set (I don't know what it is with our team and backyard play sets), and he put out the call for anyone who was able to help him build the new one. A whole crew of folks from our staff showed up to help. People willingly gave up their Sunday afternoon to serve a team member, and friend, in need.

This type of sacrificial behavior sends a powerful message that speaks much louder than catching someone during a trust fall. If you want your team to trust you, show the other members you are willing to sacrifice when they are in need. Here are a couple of practical ways you can do just that.

- *Say yes.* It is a common trend in modern self-leadership development to encourage high-performers to learn to say no, and this is good advice. When we take on too much, we often fill our schedules with tasks and activities that pull us away from the areas in which we can truly add the most value. However, when it comes to serving other members of your team, it is also important to find times to say yes. When someone asks for help moving, a sign-up is passed around to take food to a teammate who is sick, or someone needs assistance with a seven-thousand-piece play set assembly, take the chance to serve, and build trust in the process.

- *Be available.* As I was writing this book, I found it immensely helpful to get the input of others. I would walk out of my office, find someone nearby, and say, "Got a minute?" I would read them a section to get their thoughts, ask a question about content, or just think out loud with them to clear the cobwebs. One time I asked a team member to walk laps outside our office while I read through an entire chapter and got feedback bit by bit. Those little moments added immense value to me, but I know it meant the people I was talking to lost time on other important work they were doing. In those moments they sacrificed for me, and I noticed; they were available. Each of those conversations was a small sacrifice that made a deposit into our trust account, and our bond got a little stronger. Make time to be available.

Consistency

I (Rusty) love outdoor adventures such as backpacking, mountain biking, hiking, adventure racing, running, or whatever else comes along. I enjoy getting outside of my normal routine, challenging myself in new ways, and experiencing the world around me. One of the things that I have learned through my passion for adventure is the importance of having the right gear. The last thing you want when you are in a remote outdoor setting is a busted or useless piece of gear that fails when you need it most.

It is no good to be wearing shorts that chafe, managing broken buckles, or being cold and wet because your "waterproof" rain jacket was not quite what its manufacturer claimed it to be. For that reason (and because I am just a little bit particular), I will spend quite a bit of time researching different products before I select and purchase. I'll survey what is on the market and then read reviews from others who have used the item.

Once I buy a new piece of gear, I try to take it out and use it on smaller adventures before using it in a race or a larger adventure where the stakes are higher. I need to know if it works, how it works, and whether it will get the job done when the time comes. In short, I need to know if this is a piece of gear I can trust.

This process of selecting gear for an adventure is illustrative of the way trust works with teammates as well. I can't fully trust a piece of gear until I have read and heard the experience of others and experienced it myself. The manufacturer can say, "Trust us, this gear will perform as expected," but ultimately it will be my experience with the product, or the experience of people I trust, that will determine my assessment.

The same is true in teams. You can say "trust me," but if you are inconsistent in your work, commonly late in your delivery, or lazy when it comes to action items, trust between you and the other members of the team will be low. You can say "I care about this team," but if you don't invest in relationships or regularly demonstrate care to others, your words won't carry much weight.

In chapter 3, we talked about the importance of owning your role, serving your team by taking full ownership of all entrusted to you. Not only does that type of personal responsibility create value by helping the team accomplish its purpose, it is also a critical component in building trust. If you make a habit of consistently producing timely, quality work, people will trust you to deliver. This takes discipline.

We all like to think of ourselves as trustworthy, but when we are tired, distracted, or busy with other projects, it is easy to start letting action items drop or pushing deadlines back. There will always be times when everything just can't get done, but your team will be stronger when the level of trust is high, and that means a commitment to consistent performance from every member, starting with you. Here are three things to help you build trust through consistency.

- ▶ *Mind your reputation.* Truett Cathy, founder of Chick-fil-A, claimed a Scripture, Proverbs 22:1, as his life verse. It says, "A good name is rather to be chosen than great riches, and favor is better than silver or gold." What an excellent verse to live by. Money can buy a lot of things, but it cannot buy you a good reputation. Your reputation is the story told by your behavior over time. You add lines to that story every day; make sure the narrative is one that will earn the trust of those with whom you team.

- *Build in accountability.* Develop a way to keep yourself accountable to the things you need to do. It could be reviewing goal progress during every team meeting, hiring a coach to keep you on track, or using a planner or task manager that gives you visibility into how much you are getting accomplished each day, week, or month.
- *Be consistently kind.* Building trust through consistency is not only about performance; it is also about the way in which others regularly experience you. If people feel they must prepare for battle or put up their guard when they interact with you, it won't matter that you get your work done on time; trust will almost certainly be low. We trust people who make us feel welcome, wanted, and valued, so make a commitment to kindness.

Closing Thought

Trust is built over time; it is an outcome. Trust is not a right to be demanded from others. It is earned through service to them. For you as the team member, that means the best way to build trust in your team is to be trustworthy, earning your team's trust each day. You can say "trust me," but if you are inconsistent in your work, commonly late in your delivery, or lazy when it comes to action items, trust between you and the other members of the team will be low. You can say "I care about this team," but if you don't invest in relationships or regularly demonstrate care to others, your words won't carry much weight. Without trust there is no safety, no community. Without trust there really is no team at all.

Questions for Reflection

I need to work on sacrifice ✓

- ▸ Am I trustworthy? Would I trust me?
- ▸ What am I doing to build trust through sacrifice?
- ▸ What needs to change for me to be more consistent?

A Word to Leaders

The call to serve sacrificially and be consistent applies to us as leaders as well. In fact, our responsibility in these areas is even greater because we set the tone for others to follow. As a leader you will have additional demands on your time that, if you let them, could draw your attention from your team. Be careful not to get so caught up in your own work you neglect serving those on your team or keep them waiting on action items only you can do. Having a position of authority doesn't mean we graduate from serving others or doing what we say we will do.

Principles of
Sacrificial Service

Chapter Nine

Own (More Than) Your Role

In our study of the New Zealand adventure racing team introduced in chapter 2, one consistent theme we observed was each member's willingness to support one another in pursuit of their common goal. I (Rusty) talked with navigator Chris Forne, in a prerace interview, about what makes a cohesive team in the sport of adventure racing. Among other things, he explained the importance of truly moving as a team rather than as a group of individuals. If a teammate is struggling, he said, it's not a good solution to try to hurry them along and tell them to go faster. Instead, the team needs to help one another keep a steady pace, even as individual members go through personal highs and lows.

At dawn on day two of the 2018 world championship race, I got to see this in action. Our film crew hiked through the night to capture footage of the team as they made their way up the Piton des Neiges, a volcanic mountain in the center of Réunion Island and the highest point in the Indian Ocean. By the time we caught up, the team had been trekking for almost twenty-four hours through brutal terrain. The team stopped for an hour's rest at a nearby hut, and then, as the sun rose, they left to push for the checkpoint on the summit. As they began hiking, I noticed Chris was carrying two backpacks. One of his teammates was suffering, and Chris was carrying her backpack on top of his to help the team keep moving forward.

This was not an isolated occurrence. Team captain Nathan Fa'avae explained that his knee was injured earlier in the hike, and his teammate Stu carried much of his gear to ease his load. The team's philosophy was coming to life in real time, and it was becoming evident why they have been so successful. Ryno Griesel, a member of another team in the race, said this of the New Zealand team's approach: "There is no concept of individuals; it's not like 'okay, I'm stronger I'll help you'...there is one communal team concept, they literally become the goal."

Watching Chris carry two backpacks up the mountain was powerful, largely because it stands in such contrast to the typical approach we experience day to day. Motivated by either self-preservation or self-advancement, team members are often inclined to limit their efforts only to the things they must do, those things that specifically fall within their job description. Unfortunately, this means that what we often refer to as a team is really just a group of individuals working alongside each other, focusing on themselves and their individual responsibilities. But the best teams know better, and they take a different approach.

High-performing teams like the one described above are full of teammates who demonstrate the next critical attribute of team members seeking a servant approach—they own *more than* their role. Once you begin to take ownership of your role on any given team, the next step in serving well is to look beyond your assigned responsibilities *in search* of needs you can meet for the team. It is not enough to come in every day, put your head down, and knock out the things on your personal to-do list. Remember, the true value of a team is not in the combination of individual efforts but the compounding effect teaming has on the value of individual contributions. So when each person focuses only on their specific objectives, the value of the team is largely lost.

Team members who own more than their own roles put the team first, building in margin to help others and seeking ways to help the team accomplish its purpose. It requires effort, but it also brings reward, both in increased team performance and individual fulfillment. As you reflect on your own approach and the degree to which you own more than the role you've been given, consider the following steps you can take to serve your team.

Look In

So many of the lessons in this book can be viewed as simply the natural outflow of the desire to pursue Servant Teamsmanship. And that is certainly the case with owning more than your role. As we discussed in the opening chapters, adopting the path of Servant Teamsmanship means choosing to put the team, its purpose, and other team members before yourself. Our beliefs drive our behaviors. Behaviors are what we see, but those behaviors are manifestations of a deeper belief. Before you can behave as one who owns more than your role, seeking out ways to meet needs for the team and its members, you must first be open to believing that putting the team first is truly best for both the team and for you.

The call to "look in" is really a call to reflect on your personal motivation. Many of us would like to say we have a "team" mindset, but when it comes down to it, we are not always inclined to do the extra work required to own more than our own roles. It can be hard enough to take care of ourselves and our own responsibilities, much less look for an additional load to carry. But therein lies the rub. If each member of the team is carrying only the load they have been given, who is keeping an eye out for others who may be struggling or seeing those inevitable things that only come into view once the team is moving and roles have already been assigned? Who is looking for unexpected opportunities, changes in direction, and new ways of doing things? Serving on an effective and fulfilling team requires sacrifice.

As you reflect on your own approach and think about what is required to step outside your job description to find and meet needs for the team and your teammates, it is natural to think things like, "I would love to, but I don't have time. I'm overwhelmed as it is." Or, "Nobody else on the team is doing that, so I'll just get taken advantage of if I start doing everyone else's job for them." Or perhaps, "Someone on the team should help with that, but not me; I'm already doing more than my share." While concerns like these are natural, they are also exactly why it is important to really examine your beliefs about the best approach to teams. It is true you probably don't have loads of free time to fill with additional work, or some (maybe all) of your teammates will not be willing to own more than their individual roles. However, it is also true that what is best is not always what is easiest in the moment. We make time for what we think is important, and your commitment to serving the team may lead others to do the same.

I believe the sacrifice is worth it, and not because it is noble to put aside oneself to help others. No, I believe the sacrifice is worth it because owning more than your role is an effective strategy for improving team performance and increasing the level of fulfillment you experience as a member of the team. I believe a high-performing team is better than a low-performing team, not just for the team but for *you*. I believe a team environment where you give and receive support from others is more fulfilling than an environment where each person looks out only for themselves. And I believe owning more than your role is a critical component for creating a fulfilling, high-performing team.

A final component of "looking in" is asking yourself if you are willing to let others give you help. Resisting the help of others and being overly territorial with your work can be just as detrimental to the team as not being willing to assist those around you. Your capacity, like everyone else's, is limited. If you insist on carrying a large load, pushing the edge of your capacity, while others have margin to take on more, you run the risk of burning out or letting your performance slip over the long term. In the opening example, Chris was only able to carry two backpacks because another teammate accepted help. And because he had himself accepted help earlier in the race. Ego has no place in a high-performing team.

Look Up

Owning more than your role also requires looking up from your responsibilities to see the broader landscape. It means letting go of the "every man for himself" mindset and instead asking the question, "What does the team need right now that I could provide?" I love the way Chris and Nathan's teammate Stuart Lynch put it: "I think a key thing is not to sort of think that you've got a specific task but always be thinking about what can I do to make the team work a bit better or to help this team out... actually thinking, am I doing everything I can be doing at the moment to make sure we are getting a good result....A good team is one where everybody can contribute in that way and make their own suggestions or help out the other team members to essentially make the whole team work a little bit better."

Take a minute to think about the different teams on which you serve. How often are you asking Stu's question, "Am I doing everything I can be doing at the moment to make sure we are getting a good result?" Oftentimes my question, and perhaps yours too, is more like, "Am I currently doing everything I am supposed to be doing?" The difference seems subtle, but it is night and day. One question is all about me. It focuses on whether I am getting my work done. Of course, this is important and it is the starting point, but when you are part of a team pursuing a common purpose, this question is much too narrow. The question Stu posed is a "look up" question. It is a "how can I serve?" question. A group of individuals doing everything they are supposed to be doing is fine, but it will never produce a high-performing team. On the other hand, a group of people relentlessly focused on doing everything they can to make sure the team accomplishes its purpose is poised for great things.

Step Out

Berry College in Rome, Georgia, boasts the largest contiguous college campus in the world—over 27,000 acres. The WinShape Foundation, where we work, is located on this sprawling campus, at the end of a three-mile stretch of forested road connecting our offices to the college's main entrance. One day, as my colleague Cathy was driving down this road to work, she noticed the car in front of her making frequent stops. The driver would get out, pick something up, then return to the car and continue, only to repeat the process several times. Eventually, Cathy realized what was happening—the driver was stopping to pick up trash along the way. Another one of my colleagues, Eric, had a similar experience. As he was driving down the same road on another occasion, he noticed a man out for a jog. As the man was running, he would occasionally stop to pick up trash and put it in his pockets. Once his pockets were full, he began stuffing trash in his shorts! Eric would later learn the man intentionally ran that route so he could pick up trash along the road, preparing the way for others to enter our campus. Both instances made a lasting impression on Cathy and Eric, not because someone was picking up trash but because the man in both stories is Dan Cathy, chairman and CEO of the popular US-based restaurant chain Chick-fil-A.

WinShape was founded by Dan's parents, Truett and Jeannette Cathy, and continues to be supported by the Cathy family. From time to time Dan is here on campus for one reason or another, and on those two occasions, and I suspect many more, he made an intentional effort to pick up trash. I'm sure there is someone else who is officially responsible for that task, but Dan was modeling what my friend, author and teacher Randy Gravitt, calls "see need, meet need." The trash was there and needed to be picked up, so Dan picked it up. He didn't ignore it. He didn't pass it by expecting someone else to take care of it. He was looking for ways to add value, and when he saw a need, he acted.

This is the critical step. Looking up makes you aware of needs to meet, but the value is added when you step out and act. At some point, you have to stop the car and pick up the trash. You have to put your own agenda aside, step beyond your role, and do what needs to be done. And then do it again and again until it becomes second nature.

Closing Thought

Once you begin to take ownership of your role on any given team, the next step in serving well is to look beyond your assigned responsibilities *in search* of needs you can meet for the team. A group of individuals doesn't truly become a team until members look beyond their individual responsibilities to ask what else they can be doing to make the team better. Look in, look up, and then step out!

Best Practices/Reminders

- Open yourself up to help from others.
- Help a struggling teammate who has fallen behind.
- Claim action items identified in a team meeting.
- Make coffee for the team when you arrive in the morning.
- Give up a Saturday to help the team finish a big project.
- Consistently ask the question, "Am I currently doing everything I could be doing to ensure this team is getting a good result?"
- Be a sounding board for a teammate who needs help getting unstuck.

Questions for Reflection

- Are you willing to sacrifice for the common goal of your team?
- Are you open to accepting help from others on the team? Or do you attempt to look strong by doing it all yourself?
- What needs could you be meeting right now?
- Who on your team could use your help?

A Word to Leaders

As a team leader, you have a critical role to play in creating team culture; you model the way. The most important way you can foster a culture where those on the team own *more than* their individual roles is to step outside your own role to help the team in any way needed. If you as the leader are willing to get your hands dirty, others are much more likely to do the same. When Dan Cathy stuffs trash in his shorts, people notice, and it sets the tone—on this team, we help each other out and do what needs to be done.

In addition to modeling the way, you as the leader can also help by publicly highlighting individuals who seek out ways to help the team. Call it out. What you praise tells the team what is important to you. If you praise team members who do great work individually while the team is struggling, you send a message that the way to succeed is to put your head down and get your part done. However, if you praise unselfish behavior that puts team above self, you'll get more of it. And members who are selfishly motivated will find their way out of the team.

Chapter Ten

Feedback Is a Gift

From 1991 through 2005, the Atlanta Braves had one of the most dominant runs of any team in the history of Major League Baseball. The Braves won fourteen division titles and appeared in five World Series during that time. The team consistently had a mixture of up-and-coming young players and savvy veterans.

While this era is commonly referred to as the "Steroid Era" due to the proliferation of home runs and positive drug tests, the Braves were a team defined by pitching. The Braves' pitching staff produced over 1,400 wins, 193 shutouts, six Cy Young Awards, and three Hall of Famers. If you are not familiar with baseball, that means they were really, really good. It would not be hard to make a case for them to be called the best pitching staff of all time. The pitching coach for the Braves during this time was the colorful, and often blunt, Leo Mazzone.

Mazzone was known for his nontraditional, almost counter-cultural, training methods in baseball circles. Television cameras often caught him rocking back and forth in the dugout during a tense moment in the game, and this nervous tic became a signature to fans that he was locked in and focused on his pitching staff's performance. The rocking also served as a prelude to one of his many visits to the pitcher's mound. Sometimes his visits were instructional, based on something he saw in a pitcher's mechanics. Other times a visit was meant for encouragement. Occasionally a pitcher just needed to be challenged with a blunt "get your act together!" At the end of each half inning, Mazzone could be found sitting next to his pitcher giving tips and asking questions.

Why would arguably the greatest pitching staff of all time need a coach to stop and interrupt them in the middle of a game? A staff including three future Hall of Famers? A staff that clearly knew how to do their job and do it well? They needed feedback. They needed someone who could see things from a different perspective. They also needed that person to share the information with them so they could pursue getting better. Mazzone's expertise, history, perspective, heart, and personality blended into the perfect vehicle for delivery of the feedback that helped the pitchers succeed at the highest level.

Why Is Feedback Important?

While speaking to a group of several hundred college students, I (Russ) asked for a show of hands. "How many of you want to do something great with your life?" Almost every hand in the crowd went up. "Now, how many of you woke up this morning and said to yourself, 'I sure do hope I underperform today. I am going to work hard not to be at my best.'" As you can imagine, not one hand was raised. Nobody starts their day hoping or expecting to fail, yet we all have moments when we are not at our best. We tend to drift from our good intentions. We get busy. Or tired. Or stressed. Or distracted. Or maybe we are just not ready for what is being asked of us. We still have learning and growing to do. Whatever the reason, we don't achieve or become what we had intended.

That's exactly why we need feedback. It's why our teammates need feedback. Even our boss needs feedback. Feedback is a fundamental component of team interaction. Our teams cannot become high-performing powerhouses without feedback shared freely between members.

But for many, "feedback" has become a four-letter word, conjuring up images of being called to the boss's office to be reprimanded. The dreaded annual review can make the hair on your arms stick up. Your heart beats a little faster. Feedback has become something to avoid at all costs, something meant to bring us harm or shame.

What if we looked at feedback differently? What if we could take the fear out of feedback? What if we saw feedback as a way to grow and get better? What if we saw feedback as something for our benefit? What if we saw feedback as a gift?

Gifts are things given willingly with no expectation for payment. Gifts are not transactional. They are meant for the benefit of the receiver. When I get a birthday gift for one of my children, I begin with the desire to get them something beneficial for them. I take into account who they are and what they enjoy. I consider any needs they have. Then I get a gift uniquely for them. If framed correctly, feedback can work the same way. Feedback can be for our benefit as the receiver. It can be life giving and powerful for our personal growth. How we give, receive, and apply feedback can also have a profound impact on our team. But getting to a place where feedback fulfills the role it should play may require reorienting our understanding of what it is, who should give it, and how it should be given.

What Is Feedback?

The best way to understand feedback is as information to be used for our improvement. Understood this way, feedback can take on many forms, and we don't realize how often we give and receive feedback during the course of a day. A friend tells you there is something in your teeth. You tell your spouse their new shirt looks nice. The speedometer on your car reminds you to not go too fast.

While it is certainly included, feedback does not have to mean someone critiquing your performance. We have to expand our idea of what feedback looks like. When we do this, we can begin to see our relationship to feedback change as well. We will be better able to receive it. We can share it without fear. We can apply it to our own lives, and we can see its benefit for our teams.

For our purposes, we are going to divide feedback into two categories: affirming and constructive.

Affirming feedback is positive information. It can be an affirmation of something already done or an admonition to keep doing something in the future. Your boss may celebrate you in front of your team for a great sales month. Your child may giggle and yell "Again! Again!" as you push them on the swing. A coworker may mention they like your new pair of shoes. Affirming feedback encourages or confirms you are on track.

Constructive feedback is meant to help you improve in a particular area. A friend mentions your most recent blog post wasn't very coherent. The grade on your chemistry test in college shows you need to study more. Constructive feedback has the goal of "building up." Just look at the root word in constructive: construct. Even though constructive feedback is for your benefit, it can still be hard to take sometimes. It will often remind us we aren't as "put together" as we perceive. It also can bring fear or anxiety because it means someone else sees this about us as well.

Just remember, someone sharing hurtful information without the goal of helping you or someone else get better is just that—hurtful. We can easily tell ourselves we are just offering constructive criticism when really we are just criticizing. Be sure to check your own motives when offering feedback. Is this going to be helpful for the other person? Does it help our team achieve our goal? Am I delivering it in a way they can accept? When receiving feedback that feels overly critical, assess its validity by comparing it to the team's goal. Get another opinion from someone else on the team. The point is not to create opposing "sides" but to understand what is going to be best for the team.

me → Some people have room to grow in how they deliver feedback.
101 Default to assuming the best in their intentions unless you have more contradictory data.

Giving, Receiving, and Applying Feedback

There are three critical aspects of feedback in the life of a healthy team: giving, receiving, and applying. Effectively giving feedback to teammates can build trust and improve performance. Graciously receiving feedback shows maturity and a desire to be your best. Applying feedback benefits you and the team as you both grow together.

For many, the act of giving feedback causes the most anxiety of anything they do on a team. We have all experienced moments where we had something we needed to share, but it was easier to avoid the conversation. So we let it go. We stuffed it deep inside ourselves. Did that really make anything better? Usually it only leads to frustration. Which leads to avoiding the person you really need to talk to. Which then leads to awkward looks and small talk. Then come assumptions that rarely tend to be true. Before you know it, something small becomes something much bigger.

Why is giving others feedback so hard? Why do we avoid instead of engage? Some of us are afraid we will hurt a teammate's feelings or cause a rift. Sometimes we are afraid the microscope will be turned on us. How can we point out areas of improvement in someone else when we know we have plenty of room to grow? We must remember, feedback is a gift. It is an opportunity for us to bless someone. It shouldn't always be constructive. Look for positive things to share with teammates as an encouragement. It will build your relationship and make sharing constructive feedback easier later on.

Receiving feedback can also induce fear for a team member. Do you usually get excited when someone stops by your office, shuts the door, and says, "Can we talk for a minute? I want to give you feedback on something." We often take constructive feedback as a sign we failed at something. That can be embarrassing or depressing for many. This is why the proper perspective on feedback is so important. If I can remember this information is meant for my benefit, if I can believe the person sharing the information cares for me, and if I can receive it graciously, I can maximize the gift my teammate is giving me.

What if we can replace fear with thankfulness when we receive feedback? We all have blind spots in our lives, and we should be thankful we have someone who cares enough to share those with us. We should also be thankful for the affirming feedback we receive. Someone noticed us, and someone cared enough to point out something positive about us or our performance. That is truly a reason to be thankful!

Once you have received feedback...what are you going to do with it? Do you defensively think of all the ways the feedback is wrong? Do you not think about the feedback at all because you are focused on being mad at the person who gave you the feedback? How we handle feedback given to us shows a lot about our overall maturity and our desire to grow as team members. Be thankful, take a hard look at yourself, and make a plan to improve. Maybe this was the one thing holding you back. Maybe this was the one thing frustrating your teammates about you. Take feedback as a chance to grow and be the best version of you.

Closing Thought

For many, feedback has become something to avoid at all costs, something meant to bring us harm or shame. We need feedback to be at our best, and our teammates need it as well. If framed correctly, feedback can be for our benefit as both the giver and the receiver. It can be life giving and powerful for our personal growth. How we give, receive, and apply feedback can also have a profound impact on our team. We can change the narrative around feedback and make it a welcomed gift.

Best Practices/Reminders

- ▸ *Gift feedback often.* There is always something encouraging you can share with others. Look for positive feedback to share.

- *Engage, don't avoid.* Be proactive when you know you need to give feedback. The longer you wait, the harder it will be to share the information.
- *Feedback isn't always verbal.* It doesn't have to be delivered in a conversation. Write a note, send a text, make a social media post.
- *Body language speaks volumes.* You can send feedback through body language unintentionally. Be careful how you respond.
- *When you receive feedback, assume the best.* Unless you have clear and specific evidence to the contrary, assume the intent of the person offering feedback is pure. Assume the feedback is true. Assume you have room to grow.
- *Respond, don't react.* Reacting looks like a knee-jerk response. It can be emotional, unconscious, or unprepared. Responding is more measured. Take a breath. Process what is being said to you. Think before speaking or acting.
- *Be willing to change.* Don't just listen to feedback—assess how you can apply it and make a plan to change. You have been given a gift to help you get better.
- *Actively seek feedback.* Don't just wait for someone to come to you. Seek out people you trust, especially peers and supervisors, who can give you a different perspective.
- *Be thankful.* Even when the feedback is hard to receive or poorly delivered, make sure to thank the person who offered it. This will build trust and ensure they will give you more feedback in the future.

Questions for Reflection

- Is there anyone on my team I am avoiding right now? Is there a conversation I need to pursue with that person?
- Do I assume the best when receiving feedback, or do I assume an intent to harm me?
- What is my motivation in giving feedback to my teammate? Is it for their benefit or to make me feel better?
- Did I respond or react the last time someone gave me feedback?
- Do I have a plan to act on the most recent feedback I received?
- Who can I actively seek feedback from?

A Word to Leaders

Your team members want your feedback. They want to get better, and they deserve honest feedback delivered in a respectful manner. They need feedback on what they are doing well and what they should continue. They also need you to tell them where they fall short and how they can improve. They need you to encourage them. They need you to push them to be their best. They also need to feel safe in giving you feedback. They need to know you are on the same page and are committed to team success. Don't avoid giving feedback. The more often you give it and receive it, the more natural it will become for everyone.

- Provide affirmative and constructive feedback frequently, not just at annual reviews.
- Avoid criticizing, and encourage team members to avoid criticizing each other in a way that doesn't build improvement.

▸ Set an example by being open to feedback from your team. Request it, accept it, and act on it.

Chapter Eleven

Building Community

Our town hosts an annual air show at the local airport. A couple years ago, my family and I (Russ) were able to watch some of the show; our favorite part was the performance by the US Navy's Blue Angels. The Blue Angels travel the country performing for millions of people each year with the goal of "inspiring a culture of excellence and service to country." The pilots and support staff are handpicked through a rigorous process, with only the best of the best being chosen to represent their branch of the military to the public. Blue Angel members typically spend two years with the team before returning to the fleet.

The Blue Angels fly the F/A-18 Hornet during their shows. These planes are capable of flying at almost twice the speed of sound, and they can climb thirty thousand feet per minute. During the show, I was continually blown away by the things I saw in the sky above me. There were twists, turns, climbs, and dives. By far the most impressive display was the tight-formation flight. The pilots flew massive jets at low altitude going four hundred miles per hour, all of this in tight formation—only eighteen inches apart! EIGHTEEN INCHES!

Watching this spectacle, my mind was flooded with "how" questions. How do they do that? How do they not crash into each other? How do they know when to turn? How do they know when to hit the brakes? Today, I am struck by the similarities of the Blue Angel air show and the experience of work teams in action. We too must ask the difficult "how" questions, but we also must find the answers. Your team may not be flying eighteen inches apart at four hundred miles per hour, but my guess is some days it feels as though you are. Team life moves quickly, and there is often little room for error. How do you succeed when the stakes are at their highest? How do you help your team move forward in unity? How do you create a team that operates as efficiently and effectively as a Blue Angels squadron?

The Value of Relationships

The concept of community is bigger than just relationships, but that will be our focus here. Relationships are a critical piece of getting work done. While people may not like engaging, giving performance feedback, dealing with difficult conversations, or working through personality differences, most understand relationships play a big role in overall success.

Unfortunately, common thought today holds that you are better off not to engage in deep, meaningful relationships at work. You might be in competition for a promotion or new role. You don't want to "air your dirty laundry" with anyone. A boss might have to let someone go at some point. A coworker may want to keep distance between their professional and personal lives. You may not even like some of the people on your team. Why would you want to build a stronger relationship with them?

There are lots of reasons people give for being uncomfortable with relationships at work, and most of them give us an excuse to put up a wall between ourselves and others. They push us toward isolation rather than collaboration. They mold our relationships to be transactional rather than transformational. We easily buy into the American ideal that self-reliance is the most admirable personal trait. We are tempted to believe we are better off when left alone. Why do we tend to think this approach will be better for us or better for our team? In pretty much every other sphere of life, strong relationships make hard stuff easier.

Think about your closest and strongest relationships. Maybe it's a spouse or family member. Maybe it's a best friend or mentor. Don't we generally trust and feel safe with those people? Isn't it easier to admit a wrong, ask for help, or forgive a mistake with those people? Why wouldn't we want that with the people we spend 25 to 30 percent or our time with each week?

Think back to the Blue Angels. Their jobs require extreme focus on the task at hand. What if a pilot had an argument with a spouse earlier that morning, or maybe there is a sick child at home? I am pretty sure if I were flying that fast and that close together, I would want to know if someone had something significant on their mind.

Lean In

Relationships are hard, especially if you have had bad experiences in the past. You may not view relationships as just fearful or messy, but also dangerous. There may be real obstacles to overcome, but they can be overcome. Ultimately, most people just don't value relationships in the workplace. We have diminished them to our own detriment, when in reality they are the accelerator to our own success.

One activity we use to reinforce this concept is called the Wild Woozy. It consists of two cables strung between three trees to form a V. The cables are about a foot off the ground and are tensioned to allow a little movement from side to side. Two people begin at the point of the V where the cables are close together. They step on the cables, grab hands, and slowly shuffle their feet as they move toward the end of the V where the cables are far apart. With nothing to hold on to but each other, every step takes the partners farther apart.

Most people begin to bend at the waist, hold on for dear life, and eventually pull their partner off their cable. The most successful pairs discover that by leaning in to each other, they can get farther. They must trust their partner is fully committed to leaning in as well. I have seen some partners almost completely horizontal as they continue to lean on each other. Success depends more on the amount of trust you put in your partner rather than on your own ability to balance on the wire.

Similar to the Wild Woozy activity, we are often prone to pursue "just enough" connection rather than to fully embrace knowing and being known. I believe if we can overcome a little bit of fear and a lot of unhealthy societal norms, we can access an untapped wealth of accomplishment and fulfillment. Building strong relationships leads to building strong community. Healthy and successful teams make strong community a priority.

Choose to Be Consistent

To be a community builder is to first make a choice—a choice to consistently engage rather than pull back. Community builders recognize their need for connection, and they intentionally work to build strong relationships. We were created to be in relationship with others.

The movie *Cast Away* came out in 2000, with Tom Hanks playing the character of Chuck Noland. As the sole survivor of a plane crash in the Pacific Ocean, Noland is left alone on a deserted island for years. He finds a volleyball that washes up on shore and paints a face on it. The volleyball, nicknamed "Wilson," becomes his constant companion. He so craved connection he created a new "person" to choose to be in relationship with.

Like any significant culture shift, moving from a group of coworkers to a community is a big change. It requires vulnerability and consistent effort over a period of time. Tackle this in the same way you would eat an elephant—one bite at a time. Be curious about those you work with. Choose one person on your team or in your department and ask him or her a question that goes beyond the normal office conversation. Identify one need in a team member's life and serve him or her by meeting that need. Take the first step of vulnerability and invite one person to lunch or coffee and share with them a bit about yourself. Then, ask one more question, serve one more person, and share one more lunch.

The next time you have a disagreement with someone on your team, take a different approach. Ask questions rather than share accusations. Assume the best about the other person and their intentions. Commit to yourself that you will seek first to understand the other person before you fight to convince them of your side. Lean in rather than pull back.

You Can't Fake It

A popular mantra in our society today encourages us to "fake it 'til you make it!" While this might or might not be an appropriate strategy in some circles, it will not work if you desire healthy relationships. A recent survey of twenty thousand people by health insurer Cigna[6] points to the need for people to both know and be known by others. The survey found over 50 percent of the respondents felt "no one actually knows them well."

If relationships are integral to a work team, why not strive to make them authentic and healthy? In her book *The Gifts of Imperfection*, author and professor Brené Brown defines authenticity as "a collection of choices that we have to make every day. It's about the choice to show up and be real. The choice to be honest. The choice to let our true selves be seen."[7]

✳ We must make a bold, intentional choice each day to be authentic with our teammates. It won't happen by accident. Another saying, while a little trite, rings true: "People don't care what you know until they know that you care." You can't fake really caring for people. If your care for others isn't genuine, people will see right through your façade. You show them you care through your everyday interactions. How you handle their problems. How you encourage them through hard times. How you inspire them to be their best. If you really care, people will know, and your actions will show.

Closing Thought

Relationships are hard, especially if you have had bad experiences in the past. There may be real obstacles to overcome, but they can be overcome. Ultimately, most people just don't value relationships in the workplace. We have diminished them to our own detriment, when in reality they are the accelerator to our own success. To be a community builder is to first make a choice—a choice to consistently engage rather than pull back. Community builders recognize their need for connection, and they intentionally work to build strong relationships.

Best Practices/Reminders

- *Think differently*. It has to start here. Beliefs drive attitudes and behaviors; regular efforts toward building community will not become the norm until you and other team members believe it is critical for individual fulfillment and team performance.
- *Relationships are an accelerator for the work, not a distraction to it.* It will take some time to get comfortable with viewing relationships at work differently. It will also take time on your calendar. You have to view it as worthwhile work, schedule it, and follow through. Start a monthly birthday breakfast to celebrate your teammates. Leave time in your daily schedule for "anticipated unanticipated conversations."
- *Start with one, then be consistent.* Choose one person on your team and ask him or her a question that goes beyond the normal office conversation. Identify a need in someone's life and serve him or her by meeting that need. Invite someone to lunch or coffee. Then, do it again and again.
- *Open up.* True community will never develop unless team members share a bit of themselves with others. No one can know us unless we allow ourselves to be known.

No one can serve unless we allow our needs to be known. For some people, this is the hardest part; it will be easier in some environments than others. But the end result of workplace community is worth the effort.

Questions for Reflection

- ▸ Is the potential awkwardness of relationship building keeping team members isolated and harming our ability to be successful?
- ▸ What obstacles need to be overcome to lean into relationships and community?
- ▸ Do I consistently make the choice to engage rather than pull back?
- ▸ How many of my teammates do I know well? How many know me well?

A Word to Leaders

As with many of the principles and practices outlined in this book, the ability of individual team members to build strong community relies on leaders setting the right tone and creating an environment where community can thrive. There are several things team leaders can do to foster community among their team members.

- ▸ *Hire community builders.* A great way to move a team toward community is to select individuals with a desire for this environment and a willingness to contribute to its creation. While job-specific skills are very important, the most competent candidate may not be the best choice; skills can be taught. Hire for "who" and teach any additional, necessary skills. Make 'community builder' part of everyone's job description.

▸ *Create space for community.* It is difficult for community to grow in the soil of busyness, so take an intentional approach. Try a weekly team or office gathering to share lunch and provide personal updates and announcements. Establish quarterly community-building experiences and invite families to join from time to time. Be consistent and trust the process. It may seem awkward at first, but team performance and fulfillment will improve as individual members begin to know and be known by their teammates.

▸ *Model community.* The best leaders know their people. Become a master at asking questions and listening to the answers. Look for opportunities to serve each person on your team, and connect individual team members who can encourage and support one another during times of need.

▸ *Recognize and reward community builders.* People will repeat affirmed attitudes and behaviors. Over time, the behaviors that are recognized and rewarded become normal tenets of workplace culture. If you want community on your team, highlight community-building attitudes and reward those whose behavior serves the goal.

Chapter Twelve

Building Up Individuals

I (Rusty) live in Georgia, and summertime in Georgia is hot. One morning, I went outside to check on the flowers my wife had on our front porch. They weren't watered for a couple of days, and it showed. The leaves were drooping, the colors on the petals were muted, and the soil was dry and hard. Though still alive, the flowers were in bad shape, a common occurrence when I oversee the Chadwick family flora. I watered the flowers generously and went about my day.

A bit later I walked by and was somewhat surprised to see a complete transformation. Leaves that were low and listless just a few hours before were now green and crisp. The colors of the petals were vivid and bright. The flowers were thriving because, for them, water brings life.

The people on your team are a lot like those flowers on the porch, except instead of water, the life-giving resource they need is a culture where members build one another up. Through the routines, challenges, and pressures of everyday life, it is easy to feel discouraged, undervalued, and unable to measure up—to dry out. This is why the community discussed in the previous chapter is so vital. Everyone needs to feel seen and valued.

The people on your team need to be noticed and recognized for their accomplishments. They need someone to come alongside when they grow weary. Chick-fil-A founder Truett Cathy was known to say, "How do you know if someone needs encouragement? If they are breathing!"

Words are a powerful tool, and the things we say to others can have more significant impact than we sometimes realize. In the Bible, there is a Proverb that says, "The tongue has the power of life and death." Said another way, our words can pour life into others, helping them flourish, or they can take life from others, devaluing them and tearing them down.

Like water to plants, our words can help others flourish. That's powerful! When you make a habit of building others up, you can create an environment in which people outperform expectations, feeling cared for and valued along the way. You have an incredible opportunity to pour life-giving water on the members of your team by choosing to build others up.

And yet, building others up is not as common in teams as it could or should be. Too often we get so heads down and preoccupied with our own work and responsibilities we forget to notice the work of others or recognize when someone needs encouragement. We want other people to encourage and celebrate us, but we can easily become more focused on gaining the affirmation *of* others than on giving affirmation *to* others, and the effects take a toll on the team.

You can't build others up when you're not paying attention to what they are doing. Often, team members aren't making a conscious choice to neglect building up others; it's just not top of mind. I wasn't trying to kill the flowers on the porch; I just didn't notice they were dying, and the same is often true in our teams. Perhaps you aren't withholding praise and affirmation from people in hopes they will wither and dry up; you are just too focused on other things to notice that the team and its members need water.

Another, more troubling reason team members don't build each other up is they are pursuing self-promotion and believe building up someone else might mean sharing the spotlight. I am embarrassed to admit I have been guilty of this approach at times over the years, and I can't overstate how toxic this thinking is for teams. Team members with this mindset treat praise on the team like a zero-sum game, fearing, in celebrating or encouraging someone else, they will at the same time be diminished. The thinking goes, "If you look good and do well, I will look worse in comparison, so I must keep you down so I can come out on top."

This can lead to withholding affirmation when another team member does well, or even actively tearing others down to lift oneself up. But oh how wrong and misguided this thinking is. When we tear others down, it breeds competition, resentment, and distrust, all of which are harmful to the team.

When we build others up, it builds community, trust, and respect in the team, all of which lead to a fulfilling environment and better results. Selfless behavior is life giving but selfish behavior is life taking, and both are contagious. Be a team member who leads the way in giving life to the team and watch as others begin to do the same.

When uplifting words and actions become the norm, the whole culture changes. In chapter 3, "Own Your Role," I told the story of training for and racing in a half marathon. Thinking back on that experience, one of my best memories is the culture of encouragement that surrounded the whole event. If you have ever participated in a race event, you know what I mean. The street was lined with people cheering us on. Not knowing my name, strangers along the way shouted the phrase on my T-shirt to encourage me *specifically*, fueling me for a few more steps.

From start to finish, everything about the atmosphere filled my mind with a clear message: "You've trained for this! You're *doing* it! Push through the pain—finish strong!" I beat my goal by more than thirteen minutes and felt so full of life I spent the remainder of the morning cheering on the other marathoners as they came down the home stretch. The encouragement I received was contagious, and I felt compelled to share it with others!

This is what happens when you build others up. It creates an environment where people outperform expectations and feel compelled to encourage and celebrate others. Team cultures where the members build each other up are much more healthy, vibrant, and thriving, which means they are more fulfilling than teams that neglect building up others or actively tear others down.

Practically speaking, two specific, well-known ways to build others up are encouragement and celebration. These are familiar concepts, but ironically our familiarity with them may prevent us from doing them well. It is almost second nature to say "you can do it" to someone in the midst of a challenge, or "great job" when someone completes a task, but these general expressions are not likely to make anyone feel truly encouraged or celebrated. Truly building others up requires a more mean- ingful approach in these two areas. Let's take a closer look at each and how you can consistently incorporate them into your work with the team.

Encouragement

Genuine encouragement is a way to come alongside others and *give courage* for the completion of a challenging task. It requires noticing someone else, calling out their strengths, and reminding them of the value they add. When you encourage someone, your goal is to renew the strength of another, filling their soul with life for the journey ahead. Encouragement is like rocket fuel that creates energy and momentum. How amazing it is that you and I can, with simple words and actions, have such a positive impact on others. Here are a few practical ways to help make encouragement a meaningful and common practice in your team.

- ► *It must be consistent.* If you spend most of your time criticizing and questioning others, a few encouraging comments won't do much good. Scarce encouragement will come across as disingenuous and do little, if anything, to improve performance or morale. (Remember my donut example from chapter 4?) Fiercely pursue opportunities to encourage, and make it a regular part of your interaction with the team.

- ► *Be specific in encouraging others.* The most powerful encouragement is that which is targeted and specific. Seek out an individual or group and affirm an idea, attitude, or behavior serving the team well. Look for someone in the midst of a challenging project and inspire him or her to press on with confidence. Specific encouragement shows others you believe in them and what they have to offer. It feels authentic and builds trust in the team. And trust is the foundation on which all lasting results are built.

▸ *Write a note.* Writing a note takes time, and that is part of what makes it so impactful. In my files, I (Rusty) have a collection of encouraging notes I have been given over the years. Each note represents someone who intentionally took time to think about me, to see me, and to value me. Each note is an act of service. A selfless effort to build me up and inspire me to keep giving my best. What a gift. While writing this chapter, and looking back through that file of notes, I came across one that was particularly meaningful. It happens to have been written by Russ, coauthor of this book.

> *Rusty, I am so proud of the leader you have become. You have constantly taken the initiative to pursue growth... as a husband, a father, a leader and a friend. And I am even more proud of that...to call you friend.... Lives are changed because of you. Keep serving and leading. Grateful to have you on my team and in my life. I pray this week brings you great joy as you enjoy the team you have built. They have your back, and so do I! Be a team made well!*
>
> *—Russ*

Such life-giving and encouraging words. It probably only took Russ a few minutes to write those words, but their impact on me has been long lasting.

▸ *Encourage others in the way that is helpful for them.* Everyone is different. The key here is knowing the other members of the team. You can't encourage someone according to their preference if you don't know what that preference is.

Celebration

Encouragement is a way to come alongside during the journey. Celebration, on the other hand, is about pausing to look back. It means recognizing major milestones, acknowledging great work, and affirming value in people. Here are a few suggestions for celebrating others well.

- *Celebrate big and small accomplishments.* Recognizing the completion of projects, the achievement of goals, and the accomplishment of major milestones is important. It provides the much-needed opportunity to reflect on a job well done and make much of those who put in the hard work. And it's fun! At the same time, don't underestimate the value of taking time to celebrate the small steps along the way. Big accomplishments are built on small accomplishments, and both should be celebrated.
- *Celebrate who people are, not just what they do.* Celebrating who people are helps them feel known and appreciated for their intrinsic value and unique set of strengths, not just the tasks they complete. In addition to communicating to the individual that he or she is valuable, celebrating who people are builds community in the team. It requires team members to get to know one another more deeply. True community is a secret sauce that can exponentially improve results and increase the level of fulfillment.
- *Schedule opportunities to celebrate.* While celebrating is as important to the life of a team as water is to the life of a plant, its value may not always seem as obvious. So it is important to schedule time to celebrate. Build it into the project plan. Reserve a time slot at each staff meeting.

Schedule a birthday breakfast once a month. Plan for it, or it is not likely to happen.

- *Celebration doesn't have to be expensive and time-consuming.* There is a time for the big blowout, and allocating time and money to celebration lets the team know it is important. But don't let the assumption that celebrating must be a major event prevent you from incorporating this practice into your team. Oftentimes a fun treat, a team lunch, or a moment of recognition is all it takes.

Closing Thought

Building others up is not as common in teams as it could or should be. Too often we get so heads down and preoccupied with our own work and responsibilities we forget to notice the work of others or recognize when someone needs encouragement. We want other people to encourage and celebrate us, but we can easily become more focused on gaining the affirmation of others than on giving affirmation to others, and the effects take a toll on the team. When we build others up, it builds community, trust, and respect in the team, all of which lead to a fulfilling environment and better results. Selfless behavior is life giving, but selfish behavior is life taking, and both are contagious. Be a team member who leads the way in giving life to the team, and watch as others begin to do the same.

Questions for Reflection

- Do I know my teammates well enough to know how to encourage and celebrate them?
- How can I make a habit of consistently building others up?
- Are my efforts to build others up undermined by consistent negativity, complaining, or criticism?

A Word to Leaders

One unique way you as the leader can foster a culture of encouragement and celebration is to set aside time for formal opportunities to build others up. While encouragement and celebration are things you want as daily fixtures, there is immense value in creating some consistent opportunities to reinforce this mindset. Here are a few ideas you might try.

- *Unique Essential Awards.* In our organization, we call our core values "Unique Essentials." We have four, and our hope is they permeate every aspect of our work. Several times a year, our staff vote for the team member who they think has best embodied each Unique Essential in the months since the last award was given. The winner in each category receives a gift and is recognized publicly during our all-staff meeting. This award is great because it gives us the chance to reinforce our values, celebrate our team members, and model a culture of building others up.

▸ *The "hot seat."* At WinShape Teams, whenever anyone moves on to new opportunities, we host an event built around affirmation. The individual who is leaving sits on a chair at the front of the room. The rest of our team gathers around and one by one we shower the person on the "hot seat" with encouraging words and stories that demonstrate and highlight the strengths and unique value this person brings. It is a powerful time for the person being affirmed and a great way to set the tone for building others up.

Chapter Thirteen

Promoting Safety

In 1902, five businessmen from a small town in upper Minnesota started a new company. The idea was to buy mining rights allowing them to extract corundum, a hard mineral used in a variety of products. Initially the men planned to sell the corundum to East Coast manufacturers who would use it to make grinding wheels and sandpaper. The five business partners had little previous experience in mining; the team consisted of a lawyer, a butcher, a doctor, and two railroad executives.

After delivering their first load of what they thought was corundum, the partners discovered they were mining anorthosite, a soft mineral with little commercial value. With their mineral mining rights being essentially useless, the company could have folded like so many other failed start-ups. Instead, the founders pivoted to another new idea: they would make their own sandpaper. The focus of the company would shift away from mining and supplying manufacturers.

The men moved the company to Duluth, Minnesota, and entered the abrasives industry through manufacturing and sales.

Most important of all, they established from the very beginning an underlying philosophy to innovate. Roadblocks, failures, and disappointments would not derail the new company. They would simply be viewed as opportunities to innovate.

A young bookkeeper named William L. McKnight took up this mantle of innovation when he joined the company in 1907, rapidly moving through the growing company due to his new ideas and his focus on efficiency. McKnight brought a focus on quality control and research to test and produce new products. He was given significant freedom to try new products and processes as he rose to vice president at twenty-nine years of age. McKnight furthered the spirit of innovation and collaboration as his leadership responsibility grew. His philosophy of "listen to anyone with an idea" took action as all employees were encouraged to research and experiment.

In 1929, the twenty-two-year company veteran assumed the role of president and began a nearly forty-year tenure as the leader of the organization. McKnight transformed the small, failed mining company into a perennial Fortune 100 company with billions of dollars in revenue.

Today we know the Minnesota Mining and Manufacturing Company by another name, the 3M Company. The company annually produces over sixty thousand products you and I use every day. Scotch tape, Post-it Notes, masking tape, Command hooks and fasteners, ACE bandages, and Scotchlite safety products are all brands recognized worldwide. 3M is still known as a place for innovation and collaboration, and many of its biggest products have come from initial failures.

3M has thrived because it has created a workplace where employees feel safe to try new things. That sense of safety is essential in a team-based work environment. Working to create an environment of safety has many benefits for a team, but in this chapter, we will focus on two main benefits. First, safety promotes innovation. Beginning with his time as an entry-level employee, McKnight believed failure could lead to new ideas and opportunities. He worked to create a culture of safety that encouraged innovation and collaboration. He understood that if team members felt safe to try and fail without fear of punishment, they would be more likely to discover things that did not previously exist. They would be able to find creative solutions to problems that otherwise would go unanswered. Everyone wants to be part of teams that achieve great things. No one can do great things when they feel boxed in and afraid to try something new. Safety sets the stage for a team to achieve its highest goals.

The second major benefit is safety increases trust. Trust on a team brings the potential for strong relational bonds, healthier conflict management, and increased engagement. Safety leads to openness, which leads to trust. Trust is like a turbocharger to the engine of a team. It allows the team to go further and faster than before. A team with high trust benefits every team member. Everyone has the ability to grow into the best version of themselves.

A team without trust not only harms the team's effectiveness, it can also make for a demoralizing work environment where people question people rather than questioning their ideas. Team members feel attacked rather than supported. Team members only fight for their own ideas, even when someone else's idea is better. Some may be afraid to share their thoughts for fear their own words will be used against them in the future. No one wants to work in a place where they "walk on eggshells" every day, always afraid of when the next major issue will pop up.

American society talks a lot about "safe spaces" today. With our news cycles dominated by violence, fear, and discord, it is easy to see why people long for places to feel safe. Unfortunately, most people's gut reaction to the idea of safe spaces is one of skepticism. They know it's easier said than done to create a place where people feel truly safe. Many people are also skeptical of the idea because of how the term "safe spaces" has been applied culturally. Safe spaces are positioned as a liberal idea meant to insulate people from opposing viewpoints. Some argue they are necessary, while others view them as detrimental to society. Let's not dismiss the idea of creating safe space on our teams just because of the concept's common application to political correctness.

We are not only looking for physically safe spaces but places to learn and grow. We are looking for places to try and fail. We need safe environments to discover new ideas and ones where we feel free to share our own ideas. In years past, institutions like schools, churches, and community centers have been safe havens for people of all ages. They were places where people felt they could belong. They were places where people felt safe to explore and discover. Now even those long-trusted institutions have had their claims as safe spaces challenged.

What if our teams were the new places where people could find refuge from the world around them? What if people felt free to try new things? What if they could fail without fear of failure? Safety does not just occur on its own. We must work hard to promote it for everyone on the team, not just a few members. Our fellow team members deserve it, and our teams can't achieve their goals without it.

Prove It

Since most are skeptical that true safe space is possible, we can't be offended by a need to "prove it." Beyond questioning whether safety is even possible, many struggle with a false idea of what safety on a team really is. They assume this means being overly nice. They assume no one is held accountable. No one shares what is really on their mind. No one can disagree. This picture of safety is assumed because, unfortunately, this is what many have experienced. Past difficulties have brought out the worst in teams, and now they assume it's normal. When the going gets tough, people tend to look out only for themselves.

The truth is team safety really is possible to achieve, but it takes awareness and intentional effort. Safety can only be proven when it matters most—when times are hard. One of my favorite leadership quotes comes from early Roman philosopher Publilius Syrus. He noted, "Anyone can hold the helm when the sea is calm." Anyone can captain the ship when there are no waves crashing. When things are easy, it's easy to lead. I believe this quote applies to our pursuit of safety as well.

When things are going well and everything seems smooth, it is easy to advocate for safety on the team. But what happens when we are stressed? What about when resources are scarce? What happens when someone hurts you or disagrees with you? It's in those times where we must pause before speaking. We must not react with anger. We must listen and we must think. This is the time to prove we value safety on our team. Team safety takes a long time to build and only moments to destroy. Every moment counts.

The Opposite of Safety Is Fear

When safety is not present on a team, fear will take the reins. Fear is a strong motivator, but it rarely pushes people to be their best. Rather, it traps them into thinking and acting defensively. Picture a basketball team with a domineering coach. He is hard on his players and demands excellence in everything they do. His version of excellence means never making a mistake. He expects perfection every single play. He is quick to point out failure. If a player misses a shot during a game, the player is immediately sent to the bench. If a player turns the ball over to the other team, he is immediately sent to the bench.

As you can imagine, it wouldn't take long for most of the players to play in fear of getting sent to the bench (if they aren't all there already). The players hesitate to take shots. They are afraid to make mistakes because they are focused on the punishment they will receive rather than the opportunity for success. Our teams and our teammates can't thrive in an environment of fear; a sense of safety is essential. When the sense of safety is low, openness is lost. When openness is lost, unhealthy conflict can easily take root. Fear overtakes confidence. Progress is stunted. When the sense of safety is high, true vulnerability is possible. Team members feel freedom to be themselves and freedom to tackle difficult challenges. They have space to get better.

Safety Promotes Innovation

Innovation seeks to find new solutions to problems. It builds, creates, and rethinks. It discovers what was previously unknown. Safety promotes innovation; fear destroys it. William L. McKnight understood this as well as anyone. He created a policy known as the "15% Rule" at 3M. He believed giving talented people time to discover and tinker on projects they were passionate about would deliver new products. His policy stated that all 3M engineers could spend 15 percent of their time on any project they liked. Many of 3M's most successful projects came not from company research and development but from engineers who followed their curiosity to discover products delivering on unmet needs.

Many other companies have followed 3M's lead in this area. Most famously, Amazon founder Jeff Bezos wrote in a letter to shareholders, "If the size of your failures isn't growing, you're not going to be inventing at a size that can actually move the needle." This type of accomplishment is only possible when team members feel safe and free to dream about what could be. In 1962, President John F. Kennedy made a bold declaration.

We choose to go to the moon...We choose to go to the moon in this decade and do the other things, not because they are easy, but because they are hard; because that goal will serve to organize and measure the best of our energies and skills, because that challenge is one that we are willing to accept, one we are unwilling to postpone, and one we intend to win, and the others too.

At the time Kennedy gave this speech, the technology to land on the moon didn't actually exist. That technology would have to be discovered and created before reaching the moon could become a reality. There would be tests, and trials, and failures. But there was a commitment and an expectation to do whatever it would take to put a man on the moon and return him home safely. The engineers and astronauts were not afraid of making mistakes along the journey. They were motivated by finding a way to achieve their goal.

Closing Thought

When the sense of safety is low, openness is lost. When openness is lost, unhealthy conflict can easily take root. Fear overtakes confidence. Progress is stunted. When the sense of safety is high, true vulnerability is possible. Team members feel freedom to be themselves and freedom to tackle difficult challenges. They have space to get better. We are not only looking for physically safe spaces but places to learn and grow. We are looking for places to try and fail. We need safe environments to discover new ideas and ones where we feel free to share our own ideas. Safety does not just occur on its own. We must work hard to promote it for everyone on the team, not just a few members. Our fellow team members deserve it, and our teams can't achieve their goals without it.

Best Practices/Reminders

- *Don't criticize new ideas when they first come up.* Listen and evaluate each idea on its own merits. Does this get our team closer to achieving our goal? Commit to following the best idea, no matter whose idea it is.
- *Regarding trust, someone must go first.* If your team doesn't feel safe at the moment, someone must take the bold step to trust when it may not be warranted. Be the one to take the first step. Give someone the benefit of the doubt. Throw your crazy idea out to others. One courageous step can lead to many more.

- *A "protect me" mindset is not serving others and ultimately doesn't help me either.* Remember, we all win or none of us do.
- *Don't belittle others to make yourself look better.* Taking that approach will usually lead to someone else doing the same to you. Don't celebrate when your teammate fails. "I told you so" is rarely safe for anyone.

Questions for Reflection

- Could my team's failures, lack of innovation, or fear-based responses be the result of team members not feeling safe?
- What actions can I take to make the team a safe place to learn, to try and fail, and to discover and share new ideas?

A Word for Leaders

Though it takes the whole team to create and keep a safe environment, the process can be speeded up if the leader is committed to safety for all. The leader typically has outsized influence, so use that influence to create healthy expectations. Don't allow substandard work, but show grace and restraint when someone makes a mistake.

- *Encourage the team to hold each other accountable.* It's usually more effective for the team to police themselves. This gives them a stake in their own team environment.
- *Set clear expectations of what behavior will not be tolerated.* Call out what safe behavior should look like.

- *Be the model for safety.* Think before you speak. Give the benefit of the doubt.
- *Encourage new ideas and advocate for the best ideas.*

Chapter Fourteen

Sharing Resources

My (Rusty) wife and I have two young kids, Dawson and Ella. Every year at Halloween, we take them trick-or-treating, and they come home with a bucket full of candy. After they have sampled a few pieces, we put each of their candy into separate bags marked with their names. They are very particular about whose is whose. Sometimes I try to persuade them to give me a piece, and each child wants me to take it from the other's stash. The irony is both kids have more than they can eat (or at least more than we will let them eat), and we inevitably end up throwing away stale or expired candy.

Like kids keeping watch over their Halloween candy, we can approach teams with the same desire to protect our resources, guarding what we see as ours to ensure we have plenty to accomplish our individual goals and maintain a desirable level of comfort along the way. Whether time, money, expertise, staff, supplies, or any other resource, sharing with others means less for us in the moment, which is not a circumstance we are naturally inclined to pursue.

Said another way, when we focus on ourselves and our individual work, we will write our names on the resources we have to ensure individual success. But this approach to resources is completely antithetical to the concept of a team. It breeds competition, each person angling to maintain or increase his or her share of the proverbial pie. You can imagine—and have probably experienced—how this leads to frustration, animosity, and a breakdown of values like trust and community, which as we've shown are vital to team success.

On a team, we all win or none of us do, so there is no reason to hoard resources for yourself. A team has common goals, and if the goals are shared, resources should be shared as well, and this requires a shift in how we think about resource ownership.

In chapter 3, we talked about the importance of owning your role, and in chapter 9 we explored owning more than your role. In those chapters, ownership was used to demonstrate the importance of taking responsibility, being prepared, and getting the best possible result in your own area and for your team.

However, when it comes to resources in a team context, claiming individual ownership is not as helpful. When I own something, I think of it as "mine," but in a team, thinking of resources as "mine" is counterproductive. Accomplishing your team's common goal requires a shift in thinking from individual ownership of resources (mine) to team ownership of resources (ours).

This is a lesson that has really come to life for me through the sport of adventure racing. In an adventure race, when a team starts out, each team member carries the food, water, and other supplies they think will be necessary to complete the stage ahead. I have been in races up to thirty hours in length where resupply opportunities were scarce, so most of what you need is carried from the start. As the race goes on, someone may run out of water or not have enough food, or the right type of food, to perform well. If this happens, one option is for the other team members to say, "Well, I have more water or food, but that is *mine* and if I give it to you I may run out later. I'm sorry you are out, but you will have to manage because I need what I have for me." That, of course, is an individual ownership approach—self-preservation at the expense of the team. The other option is for someone to say, "I still have water or food, so take some of mine. Better we both have some than for me to have more and you to have none." This is a team ownership approach. One person may have brought the water or the food, but this is not an individual effort. The team is pursuing a common goal and will be more likely to reach that goal if everyone is strong, rather than if one person is suffering and falls back due to a lack of resources.

You may not find yourself in an adventure race any time soon (though I would highly recommend it), but you will no doubt have plenty of opportunities to choose between "mine" or "ours," team win or self-preservation. In the workplace, it may not be water or food someone on your team needs; it may be your time, knowledge, skills, money, or staff.

Maybe someone on your team is short of funds for completing a project, and you have budget dollars you could offer. Perhaps a team member is overwhelmed and needs your time to help them get back above water. It could be a teammate has hit a roadblock and you have skills that could get them over the hump. You may have knowledge that would help someone make progress or be more successful in a project or task. Whatever the need, the idea is to ask yourself, and your team, what you have that others need, or need more, and share whatever you have that will help the team move forward.

Viewing resources as *ours* instead of *mine* is much easier to say than to do. Writing this chapter has been a convicting exercise because I have so much room to be better. I have been in situations where my teammates have needed resources and I have shared with them, but I have done so with a bit of reluctance. There have been times when I have failed to offer resources to my team when I could or have given less freely to my teammates than I should.

When someone is in need, self-protecting thoughts like, "What if I run out?" go through my mind, and I have to give myself a pep talk about putting the team before self. You may find yourself experiencing a similar feeling of reluctance. You may be hesitant to share knowledge, fearing if others know what you know, you will be less valuable to the team.

You may be reluctant to share time because it will pull you away from your own work, and you fear you will fall behind in the process. You may be reluctant to share budget dollars because it will mean your outcomes might not be as excellent as you know they could be. It could even be you are reluctant to share resources because when others fall behind it makes you look better, and looking better feels good.

Remember, a high-performing team can't be built by a collection of individuals looking out for themselves, so don't let feelings of reluctance keep you from acting for the good of the team.

Growing your desire to share resources, and the consistency with which you do so, starts with focusing on the potential of the team rather than posturing for possession of what is "yours." Then, with your mind fixed on what could be, commit to being more openhanded with the resources entrusted to you.

Focus On Potential, Not Possession

If you focus on potential rather than possession, sharing what you have with others becomes less about what *you* are giving up and more about what *your team* is gaining. As you challenge yourself to rethink resource ownership, lift your eyes to the potential of what the team can accomplish and what the team can be. Two ways to do this are keeping the common goal in view and finding inspiration.

- ▸ *Keep the common goal in view.* It is a lot easier to sacrifice when your purpose is clear. You might not mind packing your lunch and eating spaghetti for dinner when you are saving for a special vacation or getting a few more years out of that used car to put money aside for your child's education. The same is true in your team. When the common pursuit is clear and visible, it is easier for "mine" to become "ours." Write it on the top of every meeting agenda, open every meeting with a statement of the goal, put it on a sign and hang it on the wall, pass it out on a note card for everyone to keep on their desk—anything that keeps it in front of you all the time. In the middle of daily work, we lose sight of what we are working toward. It is important to remember we are giving up individual resources for the sake of the team.

- ▸ *Find inspiration.* Anything that is difficult becomes easier when you feel inspired. We need a picture of what can be. We need our hearts to be stirred. Knowing that inspiration is important, our organization went in search of a high-performing team whose story we could tell. The result of that search was the adventure racing documentary called For the Team we mentioned earlier in the book and to which we have referred along the way. Ever since we showed this documentary to our team, I have noticed staff using the #fortheteam hashtag when they tell uplifting stories about what they have seen their teammates do. That is not something we talked about; it has just happened organically. Every time I watch it, I am inspired to go out and be the best team member on the planet. I see the potential of what a great team can be—the level of performance it can achieve and the fulfillment its members can experience—and I want to go build that kind of team. To become someone who is openhanded with resources, find a team that inspires you and take that inspiration back to your day-to-day.

Be Openhanded

Serving your team well requires a certain degree of letting go. Adopting a team-win mindset is not just something to talk about; it needs to be followed with action. It may require you to step out and share resources with no guarantee others will do the same, but someone must go first. Being openhanded with your team means being vulnerable, offering what you have, and asking others what it is they need.

> ▸ *Be vulnerable.* Sharing resources is an exercise in vulnerability. We associate abundance with security, so giving away resources to someone else feels scary because it naturally means we have less for ourselves. However, as Patrick Lencioni describes in his book The Five Dysfunctions of a Team, vulnerability in a team builds trust between the members. Lencioni writes that being open

about weaknesses or mistakes moves teams beyond the competitiveness and protectionism so common in the workplace.[8] The same is true regarding resources. Hoarding resources for yourself may feel more secure, but it sends a message to the team that the culture will be every person for him or herself. Sharing what you have with others to better accomplish the team's purpose sends the message you are for the team, not for yourself, and that type of behavior makes quite a deposit in the trust account.

▸ *Offer what you have.* If resource sharing is not common in your team, people may not be in the habit of asking for resources when they need them. By offering what you have to others, you communicate you are willing to help, which puts the team closer to reaching its full potential. When my supervisor hired an executive assistant, he let me know if I ever needed administrative support, I should feel free to ask her for help. Had he not offered, I would not have known that resource was available to me. This also applies to times when you have surplus. If you have a project coming in under budget, tell the team. Let them know, "I'm going to have X amount of dollars left at the end of this project. I have several valuable ways I could spend it, but before I do, I want to see if there are other mission-critical initiatives for our team in need of funding that would be better served by these resources."

▸ *Ask what others need.* Make a habit of asking others on the team if there is anything they need that you might be able to provide. Even if there are no immediate needs expressed, simply asking the question will communicate to your team a desire to be supportive. And you may uncover needs you are equipped to meet that would have gone unexpressed had you not asked.

Closing Thought

On a team, we all win or none of us do, so there is no reason to hoard resources for yourself. A team has common goals, and if the goals are shared, resources should be shared as well, and this requires a shift in how we think about resource ownership. When it comes to resources in a team context, claiming individual ownership is not as helpful. When I own something, I think of it as "mine," but in a team, thinking of resources as "mine" is counterproductive. Accomplishing your team's common goal requires a shift in thinking from individual ownership of resources (mine) to team ownership of resources (ours). If you focus on potential rather than possession, sharing what you have with others becomes less about what you are giving up and more about what your team is gaining. As you challenge yourself to rethink resource ownership, lift your eyes to the potential of what the team can accomplish and what the team can be.

Questions for Reflection

- ▸ What is holding you back from sharing your resources with others?
- ▸ What resource is most difficult for you to share (time, money, staff, knowledge…)? Why do you think that is the case?
- ▸ What do you have that others need more?

- ▸ How often do you revisit the common goal of the team?
- ▸ Where could you look for inspiration to put the team before self?

A Word to Leaders

One of the best ways you can cultivate a team environment where resources are shared is to place a high priority on ensuring the team has common goals and revisiting them regularly. Every team should have shared goals—common outcomes toward which all the members are working. As the leader, it is your job to guide the team in developing these goals and to keep them visible throughout the year. Many leaders, myself often included, are more comfortable managing direct reports in areas of designated responsibility than in mobilizing a team to accomplish a common objective. But this is our great leadership opportunity to build a team and create the future. In my experience, like sharing resources, this is also easier said than done, and I must admit I have struggled with this important skill over the years. Perhaps you have too, but let me encourage you, as I encourage myself, to commit to this critical leadership task.

You, as the leader, can also help your team by facilitating discussion regarding what resources are most needed where. Draw team members out of silos, help them discover the team's highest priority needs, and guide them in considering how resources can best be allocated.

Chapter Fifteen

Engaging in Healthy Conflict

Have you ever gone to war over a pig?

A little-known chapter in American history, called the Pig War of 1859, illustrates what can happen when we don't handle conflict well. Even though the Revolutionary War between the United States and Great Britain ended years earlier, disputes about how to divide land in North America continued for years. While most of these disputes were handled diplomatically, a few occasions were quite contentious. One such conflict stemmed from vagaries in the Oregon Treaty of 1846, which was negotiated to clarify one of the largest remaining blocks of land under dispute—the Oregon Territory.

The Oregon Territory covered much of what is known today as the Pacific Northwest of the United States and Canada's British Columbia. The Oregon Treaty divided the main part of the land along the forty-ninth parallel. This achieved a fairly even split of the disputed land, but it did leave a couple of loose strings. One area lacking clarity was in the Strait of Juan de Fuca, between modern-day Seattle and Vancouver. This area contains several small islands, including San Juan Island.

Due to unclear language in the treaty, settlers from both nations attempted to stake a claim to part of the island. The Hudson's Bay Company was the dominant fur trading company in North America, and they often functioned as a de facto arm of the British government in the frontier. The company was the first to lay claim to the island when they established salmon-curing stations along the coast.

Americans began to arrive shortly after as settlers realized the land was perfect for raising sheep. By some estimates there were at one point over four thousand sheep on the small island. For almost thirteen years, the British and Americans lived in pockets on the island with only occasional conflict. Settlers from both nations believed their nation was the rightful owner of San Juan Island.

Everything changed on June 15, 1859, when an American named Lyman Cutler discovered a pig rooting in his potato garden. In frustration, Cutler shot the pig, only later to discover the pig was owned by the Hudson's Bay Company. Officials with the company threatened to arrest Cutler and remove all other Americans from the island. The Americans sought help from the United States military, which had authority in the Oregon Territory.

Brigadier General William S. Harney responded to the British threats by sending a portion of the US Ninth Infantry to San Juan Island. Captain George Pickett, later of Civil War fame, led sixty-four men to encamp on the island as protection for the Americans living there. Vancouver Island governor James Douglas responded by sending three British warships to remove

Pickett's men from the island. Over the following weeks, both sides brought more men and cannons as they prepared for what looked like inevitable war.

Word finally reached Washington, DC, and President James Buchanan was shocked things had escalated to the current point over a dead pig. President Buchanan sent the commander of the US Army, General Winfield Scott, to hopefully find a peaceful resolution. After strong rebukes to the leaders involved, both nations agreed to jointly occupy the territory and remove most of their soldiers. Each nation left a small group to maintain order, and life on the island continued this way for another twelve years. In 1871, Great Britain and the United States signed the Treaty of Washington finally clarifying where the border should lay. By the end of 1872, San Juan Island was officially declared part of the United States, and the decades-long conflict was over with only one casualty—the pig.

Conflict

The Pig War sounds pretty ridiculous in retrospect. Two nations narrowly avoid a military battle because someone shot a pig. How did we get to the brink of war? What if Lyman Cutler had a better fence around his potato patch? What if the person looking after the pigs hadn't forgotten to close the gate to the pigpen the night before? What if there were better rules about where you could plant your garden or keep your animals? What if Lyman Cutler slept better the night before? Or better yet, what if the original treaty was clear about whose island it was in the first place?

All these things seem pretty simple on the surface, but each one could have ended the conflict before it began. All of us deal with potential conflict every day. Some of these issues are major while others are relatively minor, but as the Pig War of 1859 demonstrates, even minor conflict can escalate out of control if we respond poorly. How we react to conflicts will determine whether they escalate or deescalate. What if Cutler had not reacted by shooting the pig? What if the pig's owner offered to sit down and discuss a solution? A small intervention at any point along the way could have ended the Pig War before it began.

In most cases, conflict stems from unmet expectations. We all have expectations of those around us, even people we don't know. When I get in a car to drive to work each day, I expect the other drivers on the road to follow the basic rules of driving. I expect them to stay in their lane, stop at stop signs, and not bump into me at a traffic light. I have even higher expectations for people who serve on my team. I expect them to show up to meetings on time, tell the truth, and do their best to get their job done well.

The discrepancy between my expectations and the reality of the situation causes me to react in an attempt to close the expectation/reality gap in ways that can often be destructive. If the driver in the lane next to me abruptly cuts me off, my expectation of their driving is challenged, and I can get frustrated quickly. I can react by speeding up to ride close to their bumper. They in turn can express their displeasure with my tailgating, and soon, true conflict arises.

Unmet expectations from people close to us hurt even more. If we are working on a project together, and my teammate doesn't complete their portion of the project, my frustration becomes disappointment and even anger. How could they not understand how important this project was? The other person counters with, they were up all night with a sick child. How could they finish their part when they didn't even have time to sleep?

As discussed in chapter 11, "Building Community," getting to know your teammates well can give you specific insight into the challenges they face. A clear understanding of these struggles and genuine care for the other person can help you have more empathy if they fail to meet expectations. The focus can be on "how do we move forward and accomplish our goal" and less on "I'm disappointed." You may still be justified in your disappointment, but healthy conflict focuses on the way forward.

Unspoken expectations can make conflict even more difficult to handle. How can someone meet an expectation they do not even know exists? Picture a situation where your team is putting on a huge event. You each have owned specific parts, but in the end you all pitched in to help with whatever was needed. The event is scheduled to run all day, and the team has agreed to show up early that morning to set up everything needed for the day.

As the event goes on through the day, you already begin planning for the end. Everything will have to be cleaned up and put away. You plan out in your mind who will be responsible for each area of the event cleanup. At the end of the event, you cannot find two of your teammates. After sending them a quick text, you discover they have already left for the day. One had a child with a ball game, and the other doesn't respond until hours later. You are left to clean up on your own. There is not a lot happening tomorrow, so you could clean up in the morning. You really want closure for the event though, so you stay an extra couple of hours to put everything away.

The entire time you are cleaning up, your frustration grows. You go home worn out and disappointed in your team. What could have been a great day was now, in your mind, a disaster. When everyone arrives at work the next morning, your two teammates are surprised to see everything already cleaned up. "We were planning to do that first thing this morning!" We have all experienced situations similar to this one. Things seemed so clear to us about what should be done, but not so for the other person involved. We assumed everyone would think and prioritize the same way we do. That is rarely the case without clear communication of our expectations.

Healthy Conflict Leads to Progress

Conflict is where the rubber meets the road for many teams, and the way team members manage through conflict is the culmination of many of the principles and practices we've covered in previous chapters. While conflict handled poorly can do irreversible damage to team unity, healthy conflict drives progress and leads to stronger teams, more success, and higher fulfillment.

In our work helping teams of all sizes and structures deal with conflict, we have discovered that while some people naturally choose to confront conflict head-on, most people tend to avoid it. Conflict makes us all uneasy. Conflict hints that everything is not all right. It's normal to think—or at least hope—ignoring conflict will make it go away. But that approach is both risky and shortsighted.

If you really think about it, is conflict always a bad thing? Why do we fear it? What if we embraced conflict as a necessary and vital part of working together as a team? What if we saw it as a sign of team health rather than team dysfunction? Let's look at some ways we can change our perspective on navigating conflict as well as practical steps to implementation.

Let's start with one overarching change in perspective: conflict is not inherently bad. Conflict can be constructive or destructive for a team, but it is not something to always avoid. Healthy constructive conflict drives a team toward progress. New ideas are exposed. Different viewpoints add new perspective. (See chapter 6, "Maintaining Perspective.") Other options are debated. New solutions can be found. If we always agreed on everything in a team setting, we wouldn't need conflict to help us move forward. We know consistent agreement is not reality, so let's change our default perception to one that looks at conflict as an opportunity to grow.

In many ways, conflict is not only potentially helpful but necessary. How do you sharpen a knife? You rub it over and over across an abrasive surface to keep the blade sharp. The Bible says, "As iron sharpens iron, so one man sharpens another." Similarly, think of any time you have grown as a person. Growth only happens as we are challenged to change and deal with hard things. Conflict can be an avenue for us to grow as individuals and as a team.

Remember, conflict arises from a gap between our expectations and our reality. One way to address the gap in a healthy way is to be curious. Ask questions. Assume the best intentions of your teammates. Commit to open dialogue. Francis of Assisi famously advised others to "seek first to understand, rather than to be understood." Approach each disappointment or unmet expectation with a commitment to understand the other person. Gather all the information and perspective you can. Set yourself up well to choose how to react.

If conflict is to lead to progress, we must purpose to be helpful more than right. My friend Randy Gravitt says, "It's more important to get it right rather than be right." The number one thing keeping conflict from being healthy and productive is when we focus on winning an argument. When we want to be right more than we want to find the best way, situations tend to end poorly. The team can be broken down by conflict rather than built up by it. Do you really want what is best for everyone on the team? Do you care that the team wins in the end?

If your top priority is the success of the team, you need to be willing to be wrong. If you enter every conflict with a steadfast assumption you are right and your way is best, you are setting yourself up for further disappointment. What if your teammate has a different idea or perspective that adds to the situation? Are you willing to be swayed by someone else's argument?

The flipside of being willing to be wrong is to give others on your team the same chance. After hearing others' input, sometimes we change our minds. Maybe there is a better way. Sometimes we worry that if we don't keep defending our original position, we will look bad to the rest of the team. Your teammates deal with that internal struggle too. Openly voice everyone's opportunity to change their minds. I have seen many instances where one person willing to change their mind changes the entire trajectory of a conflict.

Closing Thought

In most cases, conflict stems from unmet expectations. We all have expectations of those around us, even people we don't know. We have even higher expectations for people who serve on our team. The discrepancy between our expectations and the reality of the situation causes us to react in an attempt to close the expectation/reality gap in ways that can often be destructive. Conflict is where the rubber meets the road for many teams, and how team members manage through conflict is the culmination of many of the principles and practices we've covered in previous chapters. While conflict handled poorly can do irreversible damage to team unity, healthy conflict drives progress and leads to stronger teams, more success, and higher fulfillment.

Best Practices/Reminders

- *Reflect on how you view conflict.* Do you view it as generally good or bad? You have to understand how you view things now before you can move to a new place.
- *Work to frame conflict as a way to grow.* Ask someone not involved in the situation to help you see how this conflict can contribute to your growth. When we are in the middle of a difficult situation, we may not be able to see the opportunities the conflict could bring.
- *Make listening a priority.* Listen without already formulating your response. Restate what you heard to make sure the other person has a chance to clearly communicate.
- *As you listen, look for instances of common ground.* Even around issues that feel very divisive, there is usually some piece you can agree on. Build on that piece no matter how small.
- *Be willing to be wrong.* Go into each interaction committed to explain yourself but also willing to change your mind on the best way to move forward.
- *Give others the space to change their minds.* Rubbing it in when someone else is wrong destroys team community and trust.

Questions for Reflection

- ▸ What are the ridiculous "pigs" I'm willing to go to the brink of war over?
- ▸ How can I help set clear and reasonable expectations on the team, both of others in me and of me in others?
- ▸ Is an assumption that all conflict is bad inhibiting my ability to engage in healthy conflict?
- ▸ Are the conflicts among our team driving toward progress or opening/deepening wounds?
- ▸ Do I consistently enter into conflict assuming I am right and others are wrong or with a mind open to different perspectives?

A Word for Leaders

It's your job to guide the team to the right decision or resolution. Sometimes we will make mistakes, and the conflict will go too far. If we live and act in fear of making a mistake, we will miss out on the constructive opportunities conflict can bring.

Conflict is healthy when it is respectful and not hurtful or personal. Healthy conflict is a sign of a healthy team. It indicates there is a safe environment for the team to tackle hard topics. As the leader, you must set the example for how to handle personal conflict. You must maintain a safe environment that allows every team member to work through conflict effectively. Your team will follow your lead in each situation.

- ▸ *Promote listening.* Ask questions more than you make statements.
- ▸ *Recognize when the team needs a break from working through things.*

- *Help the team establish ground rules for difficult conversations.* These mutually agreed upon guidelines are critical to helping everyone feel respected.
- *Embrace conflict rather than avoid it, and lead your team to embrace it as well.* It is for the benefit of the team and all its members.

Chapter Sixteen

Preparing for Leadership

Henry Ford is one of the most iconic business leaders in American history. While Ford may not have been the "first" on many of the innovations he is associated with, he was a master at harnessing the "best" to advance those innovations beyond what most thought possible. Ford did not invent the automobile; he made it accessible to millions of people. He was not the first to manufacture products; he made the process of manufacturing so efficient it revolutionized how hundreds of products were created.

Many of his ideas and innovations are still influential today. It would be easy to look at him simply as a "titan of industry" in an age where industrialization was growing rapidly. Rather than just a product of a transformational time in history, however, Ford's story gives us an example of continual preparation for leadership.

Ford was markedly curious as a young boy. He was intrigued by how things worked. He would constantly take items apart and put them back together. He started with old watches, and as his knowledge grew, he moved on to bigger items like small steam engines. Growing up on a farm, there were always ample opportunities for a mechanically minded young man to lend his hands to a practical project.

At the age of sixteen, Ford's curiosity had grown into a full-blown desire to learn, which led him to leave the family farm in Dearborn, Michigan. He moved to the nearby city of Detroit and became a machinist apprentice. Ford recognized he had more to learn, and the apprenticeship gave him the opportunity to expand his knowledge and skill.

The system of apprenticeships has been in practice for thousands of years. While "on the job training" has existed even longer, formal apprenticeships began to organize during the Middle Ages. The process involved both direct training from a skilled master craftsman as well as study in the particular trade. The master craftsman taught inexperienced apprentices a particular trade while also providing them with housing and food. In return, the master craftsman gained cheap labor to help them grow their business.

As craftsmen began to organize themselves into craft guilds, the system took on even more structure to include contracts with the apprentices. After completing their contracted time, the apprentice could apply to become a journeyman in the guild. Eventually some would work their way into reaching the "master craftsman" designation. Apprenticeships were used in a variety of trades, including carpentry, painting, tailoring, surgery, and even law.

Apprenticeships are on the rise again today, whether in trade-style work or corporate business environments. According to the United States Department of Labor (2019),[9] the total number of apprenticeships in the United States has risen by

56 percent. Over ten thousand new apprenticeship programs have been created in the last five years alone. Popular culture has embraced the idea in movies; it's shown in the relationship between Daniel and Mr. Miyagi in the *Karate Kid* and Luke Skywalker and Master Yoda in the *Star Wars* franchise.

Henry Ford leveraged his time as an apprentice to grow his knowledge, skills, and abilities. He returned to the family farm for a few years but used his knowledge of machines to work on many side projects. He eventually left the farm for good and went back to Detroit to take a job as an engineer with the Edison Illuminating Company—as in Thomas Edison. This new role provided a more stable way to support his growing family and an opportunity to continue to learn about the manufacturing process.

In his hours away from work, Ford tinkered and innovated in the shed beside his home on what would become his first "horseless carriage." After a couple of unsuccessful attempts at starting his own company, he found success in the Ford Motor Company. The company's first car, the Model A, brought some success. It was a subsequent car, the Model T, that changed the automobile world forever. It was an instant success with the public, but Ford's continued innovation of the production line made the efficiently produced Model T a history-making product.

Ford sold millions of Model Ts as he continued to innovate how they were manufactured. He was able to put all he learned over the years into creating one of the first mass-produced products of any kind. The machinist apprentice truly became a master craftsman.

Just as Henry Ford extracted great value from his time as an apprentice, we can gain similar value in our time as team members. If you aspire to be a team leader, your time as a Servant Teamsmanship–focused team member can serve as a leadership apprenticeship of sorts. The best preparation for being a great leader is being a great team member. Let's take a look at some of the ways you can prepare for leadership right now.

Build Relationships

As we discussed in chapter 11 on building community, relationships are critical to getting work done. How do you work with someone who views a particular issue much differently than you? How do you collaborate with someone you do not like spending time with? How do you build trust with someone new? All these questions point to real situations we may face in a team context. Our willingness to engage with people in addressing these situations and others will help us learn healthy practices we can apply as leaders.

It is essential to learn how to handle these situations well. Once you become "the leader," you are responsible not only for your own interpersonal struggles but those of every member on your team. How can you effectively help your team work through difficulty if you have never experienced the struggle and joy of overcoming something relationally hard? Remember, relationships are an accelerator for work, not a distraction to it.

Stretched to Grow

Think of a time when you successfully took on a challenging new assignment. Initially you may have felt overwhelmed or unsure of how to begin. Eventually you were able to understand the goal, work toward a solution, and see a successful result.

We often describe the process as "stretching" when we try to tackle something outside our comfort zone. Learning to accept stretching assignments is a critical step in our ongoing growth as leaders. For example, one of my teams was faced with some difficult personnel decisions. There was an opportunity to promote one of our team members into a new role. We had several good candidates to choose from, but that also meant someone would be disappointed.

Once the decision was made and communicated, one of the people not chosen expressed a lot of frustration about the move. He was very disappointed and felt passed over. As the director, I could have left the hiring manager to deal with all the difficult follow-up conversations. I recognized I had a long relationship with the disappointed team member, and I decided to be the one to sit down with him.

It took several conversations, but we were able to work through his disappointment. I was able to explain the rationale behind the team's decision and point him toward things that could improve his chance for a promotion in the future. He later expressed his appreciation for my willingness to engage with him and said that our conversations were helpful in getting him over his disappointment.

He is still a thriving member of our team today. It might be easy to think once you become the leader you can simply give all the things you don't like to someone else on your team. My experience tells me it is quite the opposite. A good leader often takes on the difficult project, the awkward conversation, and the vaguely defined outcome as a way to serve the team. Learning to lean in to these difficult tasks as a team member can build your leadership confidence to face them again in the future. And you will definitely face them again as a leader.

Leadership Philosophy

Do you want to be prepared to be the best leader you can possibly be? Of course you do! Then work to determine your leadership philosophy before you become a leader. Your leadership philosophy is the set of core beliefs guiding the actions you take as a leader. Your leadership style may change based on a given situation, but your leadership philosophy will be the bedrock that helps you lead consistently through any situation.

What matters to you most as a leader? How do you weigh taking care of people versus getting the job done at all costs? Do you generally work toward consensus, or do you believe in always making the final choice? Wouldn't you rather have thought about the answers to those questions ahead of time? Defining your leadership philosophy now will allow you to focus on the leader you want to become even if you feel you are not where you want to be now.

Determining your leadership philosophy begins with reflection. Here are some helpful questions to answer.

1. How am I currently leading? Even on a small project or through informal avenues, you probably have some leadership experience. Give an honest assessment of yourself.
2. Which leaders do I admire and appreciate? What do I specifically admire or appreciate about them?
3. How do I want to be known as a leader? Remember, this is an opportunity to think ahead. What do you want your future team to understand about you?
4. Does my current behavior line up with how I want to be known as a leader? What changes do I need to make to bring the current and future "me" into alignment?

5. What advice do you find yourself consistently giving to others? Usually our advice to others comes from a place of deep experience, passion, or belief.

6. What behaviors would be typical of someone with my philosophy?

That last question may be the most important of all. If your philosophy is meant to influence and guide your actions, you should be able to define what some of those desired actions would be. This is also a great way to "double-check" your philosophy. Does it lead to the actions and outcomes you ultimately desire?

Leading Through Influence

Unless you are an entrepreneur, it is rare to not be responsible to someone else. You may be the boss on your team, but you may have a more senior leader above you on the organizational chart. You may be beholden to a board of directors. In a publicly traded company, there is always some level of responsibility to share-holders. We tend to think that once we become the leader we can do whatever we want. The reality is there is always another leader or stakeholder we must be accountable to.

In some ways, we are always leading from the middle. We must use influence rather than authority to accomplish our goals. Learn to lead where you are. Learning to lead upward and outward prepares you for leading downward. This approach can also make you more attractive as a candidate for a promotion to a formal leadership role. When I am looking to fill a leadership position on our team, one of the first things I look for is someone who is leading in their current role. Who is "leading without the title" already?

Knowledge vs. Experience

While there is some debate as to whether we are still "in" the Information Age, there is no doubt the ease of access and ability to create information is at an all-time high. The average person has more general knowledge than ever before. As scientific discoveries continue to accumulate, we understand more about the world around us than ever before.

The internet (and the computers and servers that support it) has made central information storage possible on a scale never previously imagined. Search engines like Google make that information readily accessible with a simple question. Mobile devices put that access into the palm of our hands at any moment.

And yet, even with more information that is more accessible, teams still struggle with the same issues as before. Clear communication is a challenge. Effective collaboration is sometimes difficult. Feedback feels awkward. Disagreements can destroy relationships. Could it be knowledge alone is not enough to help us grow? In our pursuit of knowledge, we have missed out on a key counterbalance: experience.

Think back to the example of Henry Ford. His apprenticeship did not serve to just help him gain knowledge; it also allowed him the opportunity to put that knowledge into practice. I am reminded of a quote a mentor of mine shared with me during my teenage years. He would often say, "Knowledge without application leads to frustration. Knowledge with application leads to wisdom."

Your time as a team member is a chance to gain wisdom through experience. Take every opportunity to be fully engaged with your teammates, your leader, and the work at hand. Look to learn from every person and situation you encounter, then practice the things you learn. You will become a better leader, and you can help your team learn and practice as well.

For the Team

In his seminal work, *Good to Great*, Jim Collins outlines what he believes to be the essential capabilities of a leader. The top of Collins's five-level model, the Level 5 leader, is distinguished by a focus on team success. Collins writes that these leaders are "ambitious first and foremost for the cause, the movement, the mission, the work—not themselves—and they have the will to do whatever it takes to make good on that ambition."[10]

I am convinced teams that practice Servant Teamsmanship become breeding grounds for Collins's Level 5 leaders. Team members who learn to put their focus, energy, and will toward the mission of the team and not their own ambitions are more likely to do the same in their time as a team leader. Ambition is not bad; however it is best when directed toward a common goal. This is the heart of the "we all win or none of us do" attitude.

In the last twenty years, I have worked with thousands of leaders from all across the globe. I have yet to meet a great leader who was a bad team member. That is not to say these leaders didn't make mistakes in their time as team members. Rather, they took the opportunity to make mistakes, learn from them, and lean into growth.

Team members who refuse to engage with their team, grow as individuals, and learn to leverage influence will rarely become good leaders. They will never get an opportunity to lead or will fail miserably when given the chance. The hard work of practicing Servant Teamsmanship will be the best preparation you can have for leadership. If you desire to become a leader (or just a better leader than you are currently), the time is now. Remember, bad team members don't make good team leaders.

Conclusion

Alastair Humphreys is a British adventurer, author, and former National Geographic Adventurer of the Year who spends much of his life pursuing adventure near and far. At age twenty-four, Humphreys set out to ride his bike around the world. After four years, sixty countries, five continents, and forty-six thousand miles, he completed the journey. Over the years, he has taken on many other epic challenges—trekking a thousand miles across the Empty Quarter desert and rowing across the Atlantic Ocean, just to name two. He is no stranger to difficult journeys. Interestingly, though, of all the challenging moments he has surely had on adventures over the years, Humphreys claims the hardest thing he has ever done was pedaling away from his doorstep, leaving behind all that was easy and normal, and setting off into the unknown to circle the world on his bike. For Humphreys, the lesson is "that the hardest part of most adventures is summoning the nerve to begin, to just make it happen."[11] It is a lesson Humphreys connects to the Scandinavian phrase the "doorstep mile," meaning the hardest part of a journey is the first mile—the start.

Consistently living out the principles in this book may seem like a daunting task, but remember the hardest part is overcoming the barrier to begin—the doorstep mile. Having read this book, you are well equipped to practice Servant Teamsmanship, to be someone who puts the interests of the team and its members before your own interests. Now comes the hardest part: leaving behind the "me first" approach that often comes so naturally for us all and taking a step into the unknown world of serving others, and serving the team. It won't always be easy, but things worth doing rarely are. And with each step it gets a little more familiar, a little easier, and before long you will realize that putting team before self is not only good for the team but also fulfilling and productive for you.

We all win or none of us do. Go build a team where purposes are accomplished and people are fulfilled. Serve your team and create value for others. Practice Servant Teamsmanship, and help others do the same. Take the first step, then the next, and the next. You, and your team, will be glad you did.

A Final Word for Leaders

At the end of most chapters in this book, we have had a brief word for leaders. As we close the book, we want to spend a few pages addressing the applicability of this content for leaders and how they can use this content to help develop their teams.

In my (Rusty) early days as a leader at WinShape Teams, I found myself struggling to make the transition from team member to leader. I knew how to take on a project, give it my best, and produce a good result, but I found it more difficult to lead others to do the same. As I was navigating those new responsibilities, my supervisor taught me an important lesson: "What got you here won't get you there." He meant the skills that made me successful as an individual contributor would not necessarily make me successful as a leader.

Leadership skills were different, and if I tried to apply the same approach to my new role I had used in my previous one, I would miss the mark. He was right. Leadership required new skills, and I had to learn a new way to work. However, though leaders do need skills other team members do not, there are also many things equally relevant for both, and that is the case with the principles described throughout the pages of this book.

A team-first, "we all win or none of us do" mindset and the pillars of personal excellence and sacrificial service apply to both team members and to leaders. As a leader it is easy to be tempted to view your position as an opportunity to advance yourself and your own agenda. You've worked hard and earned your spot, and now it is your turn to get your way—right?

Wrong. This self-serving mindset creates just as much dysfunction and frustration when it comes from the leader as it does when it is displayed by the members of the team. Leadership is a privilege, and when someone entrusts you with the chance to lead, serving others in your new role must be the priority.

Much has been written on the topic of servant leadership. It is the approach we champion and strive to employ. We believe the best leaders are servant leaders. However, servant leadership starts with Servant Teamsmanship, and the principles of Servant Teamsmanship don't expire when you get a promotion. As you endeavor to lead well, let us challenge you to adopt and model the Servant Teamsmanship mindset and lead your team to do the same.

Adopt the Servant Teamsmanship Mindset

As the leader of the team, you are also a member of the team. So the first step toward serving in your role is to decide you will lead *for your team*, not for yourself. As the leader, you more than anyone will have a desire to see your team's purpose accomplished and its people fulfilled, and the best way to ensure this happens is to put the interests of the team before your own interests.

This requires you to ask yourself some hard questions about your motivation for leading and your willingness to sacrifice for others. There is a passage in the Bible that says, "Do nothing out of selfish ambition or vain conceit. Rather, in humility value others above yourselves, not looking to your own interests, but also to the interests of others." (Philippians 2:3-4) This is a challenging call, but one that bears much fruit. Something I find helpful to think about is what I want from my own leader. Would I rather follow someone who is serving him or herself or someone who is working for the common goal of the team?

Establish a Servant Teamsmanship Philosophy for Your Team

Having adopted a Servant Teamsmanship mindset yourself, it is your role as a leader to challenge your team to do the same. You can't choose the mindset each of your team members will select, but you can make it clear your team is one where team-first behavior is the expectation. This starts with communicating your philosophy to the team. Share with them your expectation that this will be a team where members commit to both personal excellence and sacrificial service: putting the team first.

In addition to communicating this expectation, establishing this philosophy as the team's approach also means selecting individuals to join the team who already demonstrate a servant-minded approach. When you interview prospective members, ask them to tell you of a time in their life when they sacrificed for the sake of someone else. Tell them your team's philosophy and ask them to tell you what it means to them to serve on a team taking that approach.

Model Personal Excellence and Sacrificial Service

It doesn't do any good to claim a Servant Teamsmanship approach and then fail to model the behaviors of personal excellence and sacrificial service. Mark Miller, VP of High-Performance Leadership at Chick-fil-A, makes a habit of saying, *trainee* "People always watch the leader." Your team is looking to you for clues, and your behavior tells the team what you really think is important.

Modeling Servant Teamsmanship for your team has two benefits. First, it tells the team you mean what you say. You are walking the talk. No one on your team will be fooled if you ask them to put the team's interests first and then go about your work in a self-serving way.

Modeling team-first behavior tells your team, "I value this. This is important. I believe this is the best way to accomplish our purpose and find fulfillment in this team."

Second, modeling this behavior serves as an example for other team members who need help learning to align their behavior with a Servant Teamsmanship approach. I remember the first time I started really asking what it meant to be a servant leader. I knew I valued that approach, but I wondered, "What does that look like in my day-to-day? How does that affect the way I lead tomorrow's meeting or how I respond when someone knocks on my door and says, 'You got a minute?'"

I needed some help. Your team may be in the same boat, and they are looking to you to help show them the way. Make sure you are setting a good example.

Use This Book as a Guide with Your Team

As we set out to write this book, one of our greatest hopes was that it could serve as a guide and a tool for leaders to help every member of their team adopt a Servant Teamsmanship approach and begin to behave accordingly. Though this book is primarily written to the individual team member, imagine how much more valuable it could be if every member of your team was processing these same things together, working as one to grow into a high-performance team of members, committed to serving the common goal first.

Team development may seem like that thing you will do when things slow down, but things rarely ever slow down. And even if they did, you will never build a high-performing team by putting in a little time in the margins. It takes intentional, focused effort, but it is so worth it. It is worth it to watch your team accomplish its purpose and to see your team members fulfilled in the process.

There are many ways you could use this book with your team, but here I will suggest three options that might get you started. The first option is the most robust but also the one likely to create the most lasting impact. The other two are scaled-down versions that are less time-consuming but also less in-depth, so there is a tradeoff. Choose the approach that best suits your team and your current season. Obviously, the bigger your investment, the more benefit you are likely to gain, but the best approach is the one you will actually do.

Option 1

The most in-depth and likely most effective approach is to set aside dedicated time to study the book as a team. This "book club" approach will give your team space to engage with the content, discuss it together, and make specific application to their individual roles and to the team as a unit.

As the leader, you could facilitate this yourself or you could invite someone outside the team to facilitate discussion for you. You could also invite a member of the team to facilitate and could even rotate facilitators each session. Give everyone a copy of the book, set up a recurring meeting, and let the team know which chapters to read for each time you meet.

You could schedule these meetings weekly, biweekly, or even monthly, though I wouldn't suggest anything less frequent than monthly. If you go too long between sessions, it is easy to lose momentum and it feels like you are starting over each time. As you gather with your team, here are a few suggestions to make the time more valuable.

- ▸ *Start with some inspiration.* As you know from reading the book yourself, Servant Teamsmanship requires sacrifice. As you start this journey with your team, take time at the start to lift their eyes to what could be. Paint them a picture of a preferred future and give them a reason to take that first step. As I mentioned in chapter 14 on sharing resources, our team produced a documentary titled For the Team that is designed to show teams what is possible. Perhaps this can be a resource for your team.
- ▸ *Challenge your team to lean in to the discussion.* Many of the topics in this book are likely to raise a few eyebrows

or even draw some disagreement. Team members may have difficulty buying in to a Servant Teamsmanship mindset. Some may not want to own more than their role, share resources, or do what it takes to build true community. Allow people to share those disagreements and talk openly with each other. Growth won't happen overnight, and you don't have to force it. The more authentic the discussion, the more effective your time will be.

▸ *Promote a safe environment.* We discussed this in depth in chapter 13, so I won't say much more here except to emphasize the importance of creating a safe environment for this discussion.

Option 2

This is very similar to option 1, but instead of setting aside a dedicated meeting for this purpose, you simply work your discussion into an existing team meeting. For example, if you were going through the book with your leadership team and you typically meet once a week, just carve out fifteen to twenty minutes during each meeting to discuss the week's reading. This is a great way to engage the book without adding an additional meeting to everyone's schedule. The suggestions above still apply, but the amount of discussion will probably be a bit lighter due to time.

Option 3

The easiest approach to take is to simply give everyone on your team a copy and invite them to read it on their own. This gets the content into their hands, and it creates some common ground you can use for discussion when issues related to the book's topics come up. This approach requires very little time and allows everyone to move at their own pace.

You lose out on the team discussion (which is a big loss), and it makes it easier for some to opt out (there is accountability when you read it together), but it is a good option if the others don't seem viable. One way to help this approach get a little more agency is to bring the content of the book into your one-on-one check-ins with team members. As they read individually, ask them what they are learning, what they are questioning, and how they are applying what they have learned.

Gratitudes

Team Work is dedicated to the entire WinShape Teams staff for their help and support in writing the book, as well as the fact that its teachings reflect shared learning of which we are the messengers. Thanks to Eric Cone, Jesse Parrish, Ben Woodard, Joseph Cook, Chris Auger, Harrison Earp, Mark Suroviec, Bradley Joseph, David Lillie, Teddy Sanders, Sarah Grizzard, Jessie Belcher, Deanna Morgan, and Jessie Morales. A special thanks to Lisa Oates for all her help in producing and marketing the book.

We are full of gratitude for our wives and children (Russ—Rana, Ryker, Ridgely, and Rhettford; Rusty—Bekah, Dawson, and Ella) for their support and understanding through the long process of producing this book. May our families always be the healthiest teams in our lives.

We are grateful for the many friends and partners who have helped in significant ways. Your guidance and support have been invaluable.

To Lee Hogan, Sarah Beth McCloud, and Derek Maloy of the WinShape Foundation branding and marketing team for brand guidance, strategic marketing, and strategy.

To the team at Story First Creative Agency and Everett Reiff from WinShape for video production.

To the team at Whiteboard for developing the book website.

To Joe Cavazos, designer, for the cover art.

To Matchstic for branding and cover art consultation.

To Mark Miller of Chick-fil-A for his influence on our thinking about teams and his ever gracious advice.

To Nathan Burchfiel and Christian Pinkston of Pinkston for guidance every step of the way.

To Gary Terashita and the team at Fidelis for their gracious support throughout.

To Ashley Roberson for helping us put it all together.

We are grateful for the WinShape Foundation and their work to transform lives every day. We are inspired by how these teams serve so many. May their impact continue to change generations.

We are grateful for Chick-fil-A and the Cathy family. Their generosity enables us to serve teams around the world.

Finally, we are grateful for the many healthy teams and team members around the world who live out these principles daily. May their example be an encouragement to others in their pursuit of Servant Teamsmanship.

Endnotes

1 *Remember the Titans*, Jerry Bruckheimer Films, Run It Up Productions Inc., Technical Black, Walt Disney Pictures, 2000.

2 Jon R. Katzenbach and Douglas K. Smith, *The Wisdom of Teams: Creating the High-Performance Organization* (Boston: Harvard Business Review Press, 2015).

3 Joseph Luft, *Of Human Interaction* (Mountain View, CA: Mayfield Publishing Co., 1969).

4 David McCullough, *Truman* (New York: Simon & Schuster, 1992), p. 324.

5 McCullough, *Truman*, p. 353.

6 "Loneliness Is at Epidemic Levels in America," Cigna, https://www.cigna.com/about-us/newsroom/studies-and-reports/combatting-loneliness/.

7 Brené Brown, *The Gifts of Imperfection* (Center City, MN: Hazelden Publishing, 2010).

8 Patrick Lencioni, *The Five Dysfunctions of a Team* (San Francisco: Jossey-Bass, 2002).

9 "Data and Statistics–ETA," U.S. Department of Labor, https://www.doleta.gov/oa/data_statistics.cfm.

10 Jim Collins, *Good to Great* (New York: NYHarperBusiness, 2001).

11 Alastair Humphreys, "The Doorstep Mile," *Alastair Humphreys: Living Adventurously*, Accessed June, 2015, https://alastairhumphreys.com/hardest.

About the Authors

 **Russ Sarratt** is the Senior Director of Leadership for WinShape Foundation. Along with leading teams and developing programs for WinShape, Russ writes, speaks, and has taught over 20,000 people worldwide with companies such as Chick-fil-A, Regions Bank, Georgia Power, Nabisco, Mattress Firm, and Shaw Industries. Russ holds a master's degree in Organizational Leadership from Gonzaga University. He lives in Mount Berry, Georgia with his wife Rana, and their three children—Ryker, Ridgely, and Rhettford.

 **Rusty Chadwick** is the Director of WinShape Teams, where he has served since 2010. In addition to leading WinShape Teams, Rusty also speaks, writes, and creates development experiences for teams and leaders. He is an executive producer of *For the Team*, a documentary on team performance in the grueling endurance sport of adventure racing. Rusty holds a master's degree in management and leadership from Liberty University. He lives in Rome, Georgia with his wife Bekah, and their two children—Dawson and Ella.